Novel Characters

In Memory of Barbara Rietveld

Novel Characters

A Genealogy

Maria DiBattista

WILEY-BLACKWELL
A John Wiley & Sons, Ltd., Publication

This edition first published 2010

Blackwell Publishing was acquired by John Wiley & Sons in February 2007. Blackwell's publishing program has been merged with Wiley's global Scientific, Technical, and Medical business to form Wiley-Blackwell.

Registered Office
John Wiley & Sons Ltd, The Atrium, Southern Gate, Chichester, West Sussex, PO19 8SQ, United Kingdom

Editorial Offices
350 Main Street, Malden, MA 02148-5020, USA
9600 Garsington Road, Oxford, OX4 2DQ, UK
The Atrium, Southern Gate, Chichester, West Sussex, PO19 8SQ, UK

For details of our global editorial offices, for customer services, and for information about how to apply for permission to reuse the copyright material in this book please see our website at www.wiley.com/wiley-blackwell.

Library of Congress Cataloging-in-Publication Data

DiBattista, Maria, 1947–
Novel characters : a genealogy / Maria DiBattista.
p. cm.
ISBN 978-1-4051-5951-7
1. Fiction–History and criticism. 2. Characters and characteristics in literature. I. Title.
PN3341.D53 2010
809.3'927–dc22

2010016556

A catalogue record for this book is available from the British Library.

Set in 10.5/13.5pt Palatino by SPi Publisher Services, Pondicherry, India
Printed in Singapore

1 2010

Contents

Preface vii
Acknowledgments xiv

1 Introduction: Novel Characters 1
Where Do the Novel's Characters Come From? 6
Surprising Characters 10
Novel Types 17

I Wholes 23

2 Originals 25
Quixote: Or the Originality of Imitators 28
Original Claims and Final Reckonings 39
The English Original 44
Conversations with an Original 53
And Now for Our Heroines 61

3 Individuals 67
Persuasions 76
Women of Character 81
Aristocrats and Commoners 89
The Incomparables 98

II Fractions 105

4 Selves/Identities 107
Me and Mine 113
Visualizing the Self 118
All in All 124
The Final Me 131
Identities 138

III Compounds 147

5 Native Cosmopolitans 149
Native Cosmopolitans 161
Stereotypes and Mimic Men 169
The New Man and the Native Cosmopolitan 178

Index 186

Preface

Fictional characters don't exist, but we often feel as if they did. Or wish that they didn't. Mr Darcy can still make young women's hearts flutter in the age of Twitter. Charlotte Brontë, alarmed by the ferocity of Heathcliff, wondered if it was even right that her sister, Emily, had conceived of him. In the "Kugelmass Episode," Woody Allen fantasizes about a weekend at the Plaza Hotel with Madame Bovary. Different readers of varying degrees of sophistication, but all very much alike in their subjection to the power of novelistic characters to enthrall. Their responses are as representative as they are instructive: although we know them to be imaginary, novelistic characters can be as real to us as the book (or Kindle) we hold in our hand. We become involved with them, identify with them, love or despise, even fear them, care what happens to them.

Why this should be so is one of the deepest mysteries and pleasures of the imaginative but intensely real experience available to us in novels. E. M. Forster alludes to this feeling of intense involvement in the title of the two chapters he devotes to character in his "ramshackly" but sharply observed *Aspects of the Novel* – "People," a word that works to reduce and in some measure demystify the distance between readers and novelistic characters. Regarded as people, characters are more likely to appear as familiars of our world and in fact play an important part in our experience of it. Forster is careful to distinguish our interest in "people" from our interest in story. Stories, he famously observed, pique our curiosity about what happens next. Characters open up a new source of mental incitement that appeals, Forster insists, "to our intelligence and imagination not just our curiosity." That is because, Forster explains, with people, "a new emphasis enters [the novelist's] voice; emphasis on value."[1]

Novel Characters is a study of this "new emphasis" on the distinctness and value of novelistic "people" as they are in themselves and as they appear to others. My title entails an obvious, but I hope not egregious, pun, one meant to highlight the relation between what is "new" in the novel's emphasis on people and what is intrinsically or generically "novel" about the particular forms it invents to accommodate them. These forms are verbal and conceptual as well as formal and structural: the novel conceives of character in a way unique to itself; the story it tells is meant to bring its characters into high relief so that they can be seen for the singular beings they are. They appear to us as "vivid" characters as opposed to inert marks on a page. It is their vividness that gives a "new emphasis" and incomparable value to the stories told about and through them.

As the emphasis changes, so do the values, a simple fact, but one that seldom colors or otherwise affects the way we generally think about novelistic character. This is a fact registered in my subtitle, *A Genealogy*, which asserts that a novelistic character may boast of its own particular pedigree, that its formations are not dictated solely by social and historical forces, but are determined by inner necessities, among which the most powerful is the necessity to become distinctly oneself. Genealogy is one of the primary ways we understand the genesis and evolution of people, and also of our *ideas* about people and their simultaneously distinct and malleable characters. Yet despite the revived interest in the novel's representations of identity, emotions, the passions, and the moral as well as social and political sentiments, what a character *is* and what character may and should become is still very much a story left mainly to tell itself. Even the recent return to ethics in literary criticism, aimed at revitalizing the postmodernist assault on individual agency and autonomy, has focused more on the value of the novel as a form of moral instruction or as an instrument of social reform than on its representations of singular moral beings. Of character in itself, literary criticism of the present day has surprisingly little new or specific to say.

Novel Characters aims to redress this critical neglect. My claim is that the novel is the literary form best suited to create characters of real, often troubling distinction, and that indeed it has a generic disposition, amounting to an obligation, to do so. Novels are narratives that represent characters with a particular set of interests and moral outlook – a point of view, in novelistic terms – that may or may not align with our own. Unlike the epic and romance, the novel is concerned to show us not only the exceptional, but also the everyday, the feeble, or the stunted as well as the heroic manifestations of character. This is why the novel often attends to characters conventionally regarded as failures or of no particular interest. The novel is as interested in them as it is in those persons who immediately arouse our anxiety and curiosity – namely, the adventurous, the charismatic, the inordinately beautiful, the refined, the rambunctious, the intelligent, the insane. It never tires of recounting the countless difficulties that characters encounter in realizing or staying "in character," challenges and obstacles that will vary according to time, place, social class, economic status, race or ethnicity, and gender.

In his engaging essay "The Depreciated Legacy of Cervantes" Milan Kundera suggests how we might begin to organize such a history according to the logic and formal shapes the novel itself "discovered" as it set out to explore "the various dimensions of existence one by one" (that is, one character at a time as well as one novel at a time):

> In its own way, through its own logic, the novel discovered the various dimensions of existence one by one: with Cervantes and his contemporaries, it inquires into the nature of adventure; with Richardson, it begins to examine "what happens inside," to unmask the secret life of the feelings; with Balzac, it discovers man's rootedness in history; with

> Flaubert, it explores the *terra* previously *incognita* of the everyday; with Tolstoy, it focuses on the intrusion of the irrational in human behavior and decisions. It probes time: the elusive past with Proust, the elusive present with Joyce. With Thomas Mann, it examines the role of the myths from the remote past that control our present actions. Et cetera, et cetera.[2]

Novel Characters, happily elaborating on the rich novelistic materials encompassed but left unspecified by Kundera's "et cetera," will accordingly proceed chronologically from the "birth of the novel" in *Don Quixote* and its European descendents to its great efflorescence in the canonical works of nineteenth- and twentieth-century, particularly British, fiction. It will conclude by considering today's most imaginative and influential cosmopolitan fictions, novels that reflect in new idioms the novel's enduring preoccupation with creating characters that might live outside as well as within their pages.

But first, a few advisories about my own avid, alternately bemused and beguiled, and undeniably partisan interest in novelistic character as it manifests itself over time:

1. I believe, most importantly, that there is such a thing as novelistic character, a claim many will dispute. I understand such skepticism, but don't share it and indeed remain fundamentally unbothered and certainly undeterred by it. I appreciate that these "novel characters" exist in another dimension, one that can only be reached through the words that call them into being, describe their physical appearance, delineate their moral traits, report their social habits, recount the most mundane along with the most consequential of their actions, transcribe their inner feelings and thoughts. Since we know of their existence through the words that bring them to our notice and that, indeed, give them whatever life they can be said to possess, we need to attend to how they are written about. So in the pages that follow, my genealogy of novelistic character is constructed and inspired by certain recurrent "keywords," in the double sense that Raymond Williams uses and recommends this term: as "significant, binding words in

certain activities" and as "significant, indicative words in certain forms of thought."[3] The terms I propose to guide my genealogical inquiry into character – Originals, Individuals, Selves, Identities, Native Cosmopolitans – were chosen with this double signification in mind: they are words that direct our attention to the intrinsic ways the novel conceives of and defines its characters, that is, to the related, but distinctive ways the novel thinks about character and how it acts upon those notions in creating and representing them. These particular words also reflect the novel's quasi-mathematical concern with Character as Entities that find their most complete expression in the Whole Person, their most distressed but also multivalent form in the fragmented Self and split-hyphenated Identity, and their most contemporary embodiment in the compromise formations of the Compound Identity. They are terms that define characters as belonging to what we might call a specific character type or genus – from the highest and foundational order (i.e. Wholes) of Originals, to the self-directed and self-dependent class of Individuals, to the modern ranks of those characters constituted of many Selves (i.e. Fractions) or endowed, often burdened and afflicted, with a socially conspicuous Identity, to the new social manifestations of character (i.e. Compounds) that I will call Native Cosmopolitans.

2. To ensure that the characters before me appear as vivid to you as they do to me, I will sometimes deliberately revert to a more archaic typographical style and capitalize certain words I want to call attention to. These are words that may have lost some of their signifying capacity, most obviously the words that denote the intrinsic disposition, defining trait, or determining circumstances that define, in different degrees and with various levels of success, the life of novelistic characters. In the current conventions of academic writing, only the word Other is routinely treated with this kind of typographical respect. I want to accord to character a similar respect and reintroduce, if only stylistically and typographically, the notion of Emphatic response, one that insists that Character may not be, as Novalis proclaimed, Fate, but it is Fateful for our reading of novels.

3. In writing this book I came to understand that my own character as an emphatic reader of novelistic people is distinctly American. Throughout you will note my particular debt to Emersonian notions of character – that character is Force, that it is centrality, that it wants room – notions that represent and respect character as an Originating Power, as a self-counseled individuality, as a persistent (even if dreadful or lamentable) self, as a chosen rather than imposed Identity, as a Native rather than alienated Being. You will note, too, that none of the characters I discuss, even those as Original as Don Quixote or Robinson Crusoe, achieve these Ultimate forms of character. This is because I will be talking about how characters are conceived and represented in novels, not as they are portrayed in epic or romance narratives, fictions in which human life is magnified to heroic proportions and even spiritual failings have a grandeur and a consequence rarely glimpsed, much less attained in ordinary life. Novels are of this world, although the best ones persist in looking and thinking beyond it. We don't read them to encounter perfect specimens, but to learn about human, if imaginary, beings – people, to use Forster's more idiomatic term – with all their faults as well as their unique claims to moral and personal distinction.

Whether there even is such a thing as novelistic character is a question that will bedevil us throughout this book, but for now let us proceed as if there is and that it is not simply a product of social and ideological conditioning or the phantom presence evoked by words on a page, but an imaginative, yet very real expression of the genius of our species for differentiating itself into highly distinct forms.

Maria DiBattista
Princeton University
May 2010

Endnotes

1 E. M. Forster, *Aspects of the Novel* (New York: Harcourt Brace and World, 1954), p. 43.
2 Milan Kundera, *Testaments Betrayed* (New York: Harper Perennial, 1992), p. 8.
3 Raymond Williams, *Keywords* (New York: Oxford University Press, 1985), p. 15.

Acknowledgments

I am lucky to have had throughout my life friends of distinctive and entertaining character. Each has contributed in his or her own way to this book, although none has read a line of it: at Princeton – Deborah Nord, Suzanne Nash, P. Adams Sitney, Gaetana Marrone Puglia, Lee Mitchell, and Esther Schor; elsewhere in and out of academe – David Bromwich, Brigitte Peucker, Paul Fry, Lucy McDiarmid, Barbara and Alfred MacAdam, Edward Mendelson, David Quint, Julia Ballerini, Cynthia Avila, Susan Nanus, and Carlo, Marco, and Marete Rietveld, a family of born readers. I am especially grateful to Susan Wolf, who invited me to co-teach a class on Character at UNC, and to the students of that class, who helped me to think about Character the way a philosopher might.

I want also to acknowledge a sterling cohort of literary critics much (some much, much!) younger than I who have enriched my life with their friendship and imaginative readings: Jay Dickson, Allan Hepburn, Barry McCrea, Emily Wittman, Masha Mimran, Ana Rodriguez Navas, Anne Hirsch Moffitt, Erwin Rosinberg, Jacqueline Shin, Rebecca Rainoff, and Mayaan Dauber. Marty Karlow deserves a place and category to himself – he taught me how to think about novels and to believe in the truthfulness as well as power of Original response. So does my sister, Dina, who always gives me her love and a place to stay when I most need them.

Special thanks to Emma Bennett, who solicited this project and encouraged me along the way; Caroline Clamp; and my copy editor, Harry Langford.

My splendid sons, Daniel and Matthew, keep me sane and honest and always give me fresh reason to delight in their intelligence, their humor, and their company.

Finally this book is dedicated to Barbara Rietveld, a woman of extraordinary character and a subtle reader of minds and hearts.

1

Introduction: Novel Characters

Emerson thought that character was nature in the highest form.[1] He is thinking here of character as virtually a synonym for Genius, but even so, this is a compliment to human nature that few would second without qualification. The standard might strike us as too high, even out of reach, especially when applied to the characters that populate the novel, a genre dedicated to giving us realistic, rather than idealized depictions of human beings. It would hardly take a moment's thought to identify the variety of morally objectionable characters who are so much at home in the novel: weak and bad characters, for one, and then all variety of those sneaky, weasely, or weedy characters who plague and exasperate us. The name and number of human nature in its lowest form are, distressingly, legion. There is a history for approaching character in these less exalted and often standardized forms, but while acknowledging this history, it is my intention to write against it in an Emersonian vein of exhortation, urging us to seek out not what is standard but what is original, not what is typical, but what is exceptional, not what is predictable, but what is surprising, bewildering, potentially alarming, and ultimately transformative about the way the novel conceives of character.

The literary notion of character has long associated itself with ideas of distinction, although not always of the most favorable kind. The known history of "character writing" begins with Theophrastus, whose *Characters* was the first systematic attempt to describe distinct types of character – thirty in the version that has come down to us – identified by "the mode in which they administer their affairs."[2] Although a preface, which was once believed to have been written by Theophrastus, claims he arrived at these character types by observing, "side by side, with great closeness, both the good and the worthless among men," none of the good men, who presumably would give us examples of nature in its highest form, find a place in his account. *Characters* begins by depicting the "doublings and retractions" of the Ironical man and concludes with the stinting ways of the Avaricious Man. They are the first and last exhibit in a rogues' gallery depicting a morally instructive, often comical array of conniving, insincere, ill-behaved, and self-interested characters, all of them prototypes of a specific and generally obnoxious trait.

Thus, for example, Theophrastus describes the characteristic manners of the flatterer, the garrulous man, the chatty man, the boaster, the gossip (or fabricator), the evil-speaker (or slanderer), and the gross man (known for his "obtrusive and objectionable pleasantry") so that we might know them and know, too, the differences between the man who is merely chatty, the man intent on fabricating stories about others, and the man who enjoys slandering others. Similarly, he records the extravagances of the shameless man, the reckless man, the boaster; the misplaced self-regard of the arrogant man, the mean man, and the complacent man; the cramped and stunted nature of the penurious man, the unreasonable man, the surly man, the grumbler, the unpleasant man, and the offensive man (the last two cousins but not twins); the presumptions of the distrustful man and the late-learner; the power-mongering of the officious man, the man of mean ambitions, the oligarch, and the patron of rascals ("philoponeria," literally, the lover of bad company); and the mental and moral weaknesses of the stupid man, the superstitious man, the coward.

The "character as genre" invented by Theophrastus inclines, then, to satire, delineating characters exclusively in terms of their public face, which more or less is presumed to reflect – a "more or less" that will come back to haunt us – their inner and most consistent disposition. The satiric bite of his sketches is in keeping with the meaning of the Greek word, character, an engraved mark, derived from *kharas,* the stylus or sharp-pointed implement for writing on clay or wax tablets. Character in this double sense refers to what etches and is etched, what makes the mark and the graphic mark (hieroglyph or letter) itself. This etymology is morally as well as technically suggestive. The stylus makes distinctive marks through a steady application of force; so, too, character is fashioned by those pressuring forces that shape, condition, and keep character *in* character. Dickens seizes on the psychological as well as dramatic possibilities of this double and uncanny sense of character in *Great Expectations,* a novel, as we shall see, haunted by various inscriptions and turns of character. Character is literally reduced to a graphic sign when Pip's sister, unable to speak after being brutally assaulted, tries to communicate a felt and urgent want by tracing "a character that looked like a curious T." In a frenzy of decoding, Pip produces "everything producible that began with T, from tar to toast and tub"[3] until, with the help of Biddy, he suddenly realizes that the scrawled T is not a letter, but the pictogram of a hammer. Once the "character" of the sign is deciphered, it becomes clear who is meant: Orlick, instantly identifiable by his tools and characteristic activity at the forge. Dickens's play on these older meanings of character as letter, mark, and expressive tool prepares for the darker and less easily solvable mystery of Orlick's character – who he is and what he is when he is not at work, when his characteristic hammering takes a violently personal form.

The Greeks had another word that recognized and denoted character in its habitual dispositions and as an ensemble of moral traits: the word *ethos* (a cognate of the word *idiom,* which indicates the particularity not of persons but of their language). This is the word that Aristotle uses when he speaks of tragic character in the *Poetics.* It is a word that has descended to us and is still in use today to refer to the marked traits, customs, sentiments, or beliefs that define a person, a group, or a culture. The word *ethics* also derives from *ethos*. The conjunction of ethos and character indicates a primary interest in what is habitual or durable about character: a conception of character that, however well suited to delineating human beings in their most expressive poses, habits, attitudes, and behaviors is not inherently disposed to dramatic development. This is why Aristotle can argue that while you cannot have a tragedy without action, you can have one without character. Nonetheless, the idea of character as an habitual expression presupposes the idea of breaking or eluding habit, a possibility conveyed when we say someone is acting out of character, as if character were something we could temporarily divest ourselves of, like an ill-fitting or constraining garment, in order to feel a bit more free, a bit more or, as the case may be, a little less like our habitual selves.

These fundamental conceptions of character as a marked moral type or a habitual and consistent behavior are absorbed and transformed in the modern and distinctly novelistic notion of character as "a process and unfolding,"[4] to use George Eliot's apt phrase. Character is no longer seen as a finished form, but as something – a force, an essence, a psychic embryo – that develops over time; one grows into a character, realizes and fulfills it, abandons or betrays it. Such narratives trouble our received notions of what it actually means to say that someone is acting "in character" – are such acts performed freely or under some outer or even inner compulsion? Are they prompted by genuine and individual instincts and dispositions, or by conditioned behaviors that adhere to social conventions dictating what we should be and ought to do? These questions will preoccupy us for the rest of this book, because these are the questions that preoccupy the novel in its central endeavor – to represent the different kinds and the changing fate of character. For now we can conclude this brief history of character by considering the radically libertarian and still controversial view that posits character as intrinsic rather than inscribed, as self-sufficing and self-impelled rather than predominantly shaped by custom and convention.

One of the more fervent and sustained expressions of this view appears in John Stuart Mill's *On Liberty*, a work we will revisit in the chapter on Individuals. This is how Mill defines character: "A person whose desires and impulses are his own – are the expression of his own nature, as it has been developed and modified by his own culture – is said to have a character. One whose desires and impulses are not his own, has no character, no more than a steam-engine has character."[5] In an age when industrialization was transforming not only the way we lived, but also the way we thought about ourselves as human beings, Mill passionately argued that character was not a mechanism, but was an organism that "requires to grow and develop itself on all sides, according to the tendency of the inward forces which makes it a living thing."[6] Character is the flowering (he uses, in fact, a botanical metaphor for character development) of these inward forces as they develop and are modified in response to the cultural environment.

Emerson shares this libertarian bias, but so enlarges upon it that the social and cultural environment in which character moves and acts dwindles to a backdrop or must adapt to *its* imperative presence. That character can act on its environment, like Robinson Crusoe, dominate it, like Ahab, and even transform it, like Don Quixote, are possibilities the novel can hardly wait to explore. The novel tests these possibilities, sometimes comically, sometimes tragically, sometimes with stoic calm or visionary excitement, sometimes, as in *Don Quixote* or *The Brothers Karamazov* or *Ulysses*, in a combination of all these moods.

Emerson abounds in emphatic definitions for character, two of which are especially notable in isolating the charisma of character. First the definition that opens his essay on "Character":

> This is that which we call Character, – a reserved force which acts directly by presence, and without means. It is conceived of as a certain indemonstrable force, a Familiar or Genius, by whose impulses the man is guided, but whose counsels he cannot impart; which is company for him, so that such men are often solitary, or if they chance to be social, do not need society, but can entertain themselves very well alone.

And then midway through the essay, this astonishing announcement:

> Character is centrality, the impossibility of being displaced or overset.[7]

If we understand character, as Emerson urged us, as centrality, as an undisplaceable and undemonstrable Force, we can see how it can be represented to us as nature's highest form. This is the definition that inspired this book and which shall accompany us through to its end.

Where Do the Novel's Characters Come From?

Let us, then, examine the validity of Emerson's claims for character as the Force or Familiar by whose impulses men (and women) are guided. According to Emerson, character, if it actually is character in its truest and highest form, is centrality; everything emanates from it, nothing is imposed upon it that it does not want or accept or welcome. This definition holds, I would argue, for both "real" and fictional characters. Nonetheless, fictional characters emerge out of the crucible of imagination rather than the womb of Nature. Their creation is the highest work of epic poets, romancers, dramatists, and novelists, just as the Genius is the most accomplished work of Nature. Since we are concerned here with the work of novelists, let us turn to one who has offered her own creation myth of fictional character in a volume whose very title evokes the ontogenic relation between *Writing and Being*.

> "The writer is the Adam's rib of character."[8]

This striking sentence appears in the midst of an essay by Nadine Gordimer on the relation between the novelist and her characters. It occupies a paragraph by itself, as if Gordimer wanted to isolate the mysterious origin of character from the prosaic matter surrounding and threatening to engulf it. This itself is a clue to how character aims at distinction and pride of place.

The hieratic tone of this pronouncement is all the more arresting since it is preceded by more genial and personal reflections on

Gordimer's own beginnings as a writer. Gordimer has been good-naturedly confessing that in her younger days she had played, sometimes to the point of obsession, what her mature self calls "the I-spy game – looking for real life counterparts to fictional personages." Looking back on "the radiant reading days of adolescence," Gordimer admits that she is "puzzled to remember how, deep in D. H. Lawrence, I went through the local library in fervent pursuit of his circle as real-life counterparts of his characters." Her first target was the character of the famously generous, oddly mannered, bizarrely dressed Edwardian "hostess" to the luminaries of modernism, Ottoline Morrell, so brilliantly ransacked and pilloried and, as Gordimer only realized later, *transformed* in Lawrence's lacerating, unforgettable portrait of Hermione Roddice in *Women in Love*.

Gordimer not only grows out of the "prying and prurience and often absurdity"[9] of the I-spy game but actively comes to resent it once she herself becomes a novelist and starts to appreciate the difference between actual living characters and imagined ones, between the copyist and the transformer of life. In the essay she palpably bristles at the invasive questions she might have asked herself in her younger days: "What is it these impertinent interrogators want from us," she blurts out in a rare flash of irritation: "An admission that your Albertine was actually gay Albert? That Malone was Beckett's neglected grandfather? That Nabokov alias Humbert Humbert didn't chase only butterflies?"[10]

Since we are not likely *ever* to wring such admissions out of her or any other writer for that matter, our time and intelligence is better applied interrogating other matters. We might begin by questioning what Gordimer hoped to convey through this uncanny image of the writer as the Adam's rib of character. She herself glosses it by citing two radically opposed deterministic "theses" about literary character: one is Edward Said's claim in *Joseph Conrad and the Fiction of Autobiography* (1966) that "the writer's life is the story"; the other is Roland Barthes's demonstration in *S/Z* (1970) that "what is told is the telling," that, in other words, there is no plot, no subject, and most definitely no writer, hence no personal character, at all. Gordimer is quick to note that both Said and Barthes would modify and even contradict these claims later in their career. But these particular works are important to Gordimer as critical landmarks "representative of at least two of the sand-shoals of literary theory that wash up on either bank of the writer's imagination as it flows unconcernedly on."

As this last image suggests, neither the possibility that the writer is all "there" in the story or completely absent from it can divert the novelist's imagination from its appointed course. Nor does Gordimer herself seem concerned that she has not answered the question of where characters come from. She leaves the question where she found it, in the realm of mystery. She is, however, quite willing to answer the equally difficult question of what a character is: "a coherence in the babble of the conscious and unconscious, a gathering from a diaspora that does not know from what territory of cognition it has been dispersed."[11]

Coherence: this is the term – and the promise! – to seize and hold on to, as we wrestle with our notions, which most likely are inherited, conventional, and highly personal, of what novelistic characters are. According to Gordimer, character does *not* possess the coherence of something "constructed," as the social determinists insist, to conform to the specifications of some ideological blueprint. Rather, Gordimer insists, character resembles the "coherence" most commonly experienced in dreams, which also unfold in our minds as a barely intelligible babble of conscious and unconscious thoughts. This dream-coherence is a sign of its origin and, indeed, of its parentage. Adam, we are told, was in a deep sleep when his rib was extracted from him. The inference here is that the writer may create his or her characters in a kind of trance or waking dream. Certainly this is how Freud understood the mystery of artistic creation, at least when it came to the creation of characters. His majesty, the Ego, Freud proposed, is the hidden magnificence behind those stories fashioned out of the daydreams of novelists and romancers. This majesty is embodied in the figure of the hero or heroine, "for whom," Freud argues, "the writer tries to win our sympathy by every possible means and whom he seems to place under the protection of a special providence."[12] The sympathetic character of the hero or heroine and the special protection accorded them are meant to make the reader complicit in fantasies he would ordinarily reject or censure as egocentric. These wishes Freud broadly characterized as either ambitious wishes, which serve to "elevate the subject's personality," and erotic wishes. Men, he claimed, traditionally are inspired by dreams of ambition, women by erotic wishes. We shall see how the novel overturns some of these traditions, giving women their first real chance to be ambitious for themselves.

Such wishes and ambitions did not concern, if they ever attracted the notice of Theophrastus, who "sketches" the public face and conduct of characters rather than probing and excavating their private and inner lives. But they are the central concern and subject of the novel, whose primary cultural function is to satisfy our curiosity about why human beings are the way they are and act the way they do. The novel seeks this more complete *human* understanding not just in the public expressions and behavior, but in the private habits and inner thoughts of character. It observes, studies, and depicts character in its everyday routines as well as holiday moods. When the private and public facts fail to agree, as they often do, the novel wants to know the circumstances, extenuating or not, before it reaches any conclusions or delivers any moral verdicts.

This is one of the important ways in which novelistic characters differ from their close relatives of the theater. The life of dramatic characters is, self-evidently, confined to the stage, the realm, as Georg Lukács has remarked,

> of naked souls and fates; every stage is Greek in its innermost essence: abstractly clothed people walk onto it and perform their play of fate before abstractly grand, empty columned halls. Costumes, milieu, wealth and variety are a mere compromise for the stage. At the truly decisive moment they always become superficial and thus distracting.[13]

But for novelistic characters, costumes, milieu, and wealth, not to mention their work, if they have any, their habits, such as they are, their stray as well as most concentrated thoughts, do not compromise, but constitute the very essence of who they are. Even that most unyielding, undisplaceable character, Don Quixote, would not be who he is without his sword and buckler, his chivalric code, his gaunt body and abstemious habits, the "milieu" of La Mancha, and the New as well as Old Spain through which he travels in search of ennobling adventure. Novelistic characters – even those spiritually tormented beings in Dostoevsky's novels – may impress us as souls more than characters, but nevertheless, they are not *naked* souls; character is the moral garment that clothes and shields them from the blasts of fate.

The novel, unlike the drama, suspends its characters in a time and place where the play of fate is not predetermined and often not even concluded. Many a novel, of course, ends by telling us how their characters resolved their problems, found their mate, achieved their destiny (such as it is), and lived out their lives beyond the last page of the book. But there are also novels that end without disclosing the ultimate fate of one or more of their characters, leaving us, like Scarlett O'Hara, clinging to the thought that tomorrow is another day. How that day dawns and how it will end is not part of the story that some novelists feel obliged or even *able* to tell. Characters may be born, as Gordimer claims, in an ingathering of the novelist's dispersed conscious and unconscious wishes, intuitions, and perceptions, but once created and released back into the world, they may end up anywhere. Novelistic characters in particular are notorious for defying as much as fulfilling our expectations and hopes for them. We need to acknowledge and accept this fact about them – that they would not be novelistic characters if they did not possess and exercise their capacity to surprise – including the capacity to surprise themselves. This capacity for surprise is a measure of their freedom *as* novelistic characters.

Surprising Characters

My argument for surprise as a defining element of literary character was inspired by E. M. Forster's distinction between flat and round characters in his highly suggestive and entertaining *Aspects of the*

Novel. It is a distinction that can be easily dismissed as too reductive, but we shouldn't be put off by the apparently schematic nature of the distinction or by the fact that Forster proposes a duality that even he is not terribly invested in enforcing. This duality is framed as a kind of differential calculus:

> Flat characters were called "humours" in the seventeenth century, and are sometimes called types, and sometimes caricatures. In their purest form, they are constructed round a single idea or quality: when there is more than one factor in them, we get the beginning of the curve toward the round.[14]

On this side of the curve, in the flatlands, as it were, where most of the novel's minor, but remarkably vital characters congregate and sometimes huddle, Forster puts characters like Mrs Micawber, whose "character can be expressed in one sentence such as 'I never will desert Mr Micawber.'" These flat characters have the great advantage of being easily recognized whenever they appear – "recognized by the reader's emotional eye, not by the visual eye, which merely notes the recurrence of a proper name."

But then Forster's own argument begins to curve, and to take us into unexpectedly strange territories. Suddenly we are asked to look at flat characters not from the point of view of the reader, but from the perspective of the novelist who seems, at least to me, unusually eager to impress us with his own creative force of character: "It is a convenience for an author when he can strike with his full force at once, and flat characters are very useful to him, since they never need reintroducing, never run away, have not to be watched for development, and provide their own atmosphere – little luminous disks of a pre-arranged size, pushed hither and thither like counters across the void or between the stars; most satisfactory."[15] Forster, in most instances the most amiable of writers, gives us a rare glimpse of a more grandiose and despotic side to his character as a novelist, if not as a human being, in elaborating this image of the author as the demiurgic power within the universe he calls into existence.

This is a much more unsettling picture of the novelist than Gordimer's image of the writer as the Adam's rib of character. Forster portrays the novelist as an ever-wakeful creator, carefully monitoring those characters who might foil his design, run away with his themes, step out of their own atmosphere, and make their own way in the void or the space between the stars. Much depends, of course, on whether you think Forster is talking to us or to himself when, in summarizing the various "conveniences" of flat characters, he comments, as if in a stage whisper, "most satisfactory." Is this the satisfaction the novelist feels in exercising his unopposed power to treat his flat characters as counters that have predetermined natures and predestined uses? Or does it signal the special satisfaction he feels in the more magnificent if ambiguous accomplishment of securing for even the flattest and least remarkable of his characters a place among the stars?

Apart from this odd and somewhat unnerving digression into the novelist's own mental space, these remarks on flat characters will strike most readers as sensible and, indeed, intuitively right. We can easily spot those characters destined to remain flat, never to curve into the round, characters who, because they have no appreciable contour to them, do not arouse our anxiety or curiosity. We know who they are right away and know, too, that what we see is pretty much all there is to them. This is the feeling C. K. Dexter Haven conveys to his ex-wife Tracy Lord in *The Philadelphia Story* when he objects to the character of George Kittredge, the man she is about to marry, as unworthy of her. When Tracy, at once defiant and defensive, retorts "You hardly know him," Dexter immediately counters: "To hardly know him is to know him well." I hardly know a better way to describe a flat character.

Flat characters like George Kittredge may be, as they are to C. K. Dexter Haven, a source of irritation, or, more typically, of comic relief; they can even make us shudder with their shallow villainy or moral obtuseness, but they are not really meant to baffle and discompose us. To hardly know them is to know them well. The same can't be said of round characters. This is how Forster describes them: "The test of a round character is whether it is capable of surprising in a convincing way. If it never surprises it is flat. If it does not convince, it is a flat pretending to be round. It has the incalculability of life about it – life within the pages of a book."[16] Round characters are more contoured, have a volume and dimensions that prevent us from seeing round them. They are incalculable, elude our reckoning; they are, as Forster might say, terribly inconvenient in refusing to act in consistent and predictable ways. We feel our knowledge of them is less stable and complete than that offered by flat characters who, like Theophrastus's characters, never vary or stray from themselves. At the same time, they seem to offer a new understanding of human nature, less systematic, but more concrete and more attuned to the hard-to-reach or seldom-seen inner life of character.

This is the new kind of knowledge that the novel was invented to procure and make available for human use. Novelists experimented with the devices of first and third person, unreliable and omniscient narrators and invented specific techniques, like free indirect discourse and stream of consciousness, to show us the inner life as well outward expression of character. These techniques were designed to put us into closer contact with the presence that acts upon us, as Emerson says, without means. This relatively new and importunate need to reckon with the moral unpredictability of "rounded" character is presaged in the figure and predicament of Hamlet. Hamlet is the dramatic character who mediates between the classical sense of character as *ethos*, known by its habitual dispositions and identifiable traits, and the modern, by which I mean post-Romantic, sense of character as presence and force. When Hamlet warns Laertes, "Yet I have in me something dangerous which let thy wisdom fear," (V, I, 262–65), he is anticipating this modern sense of character. It is precisely this sense of his own character as a reserved Force, indeed as an incalculable, potentially dangerous Force, that makes Hamlet a threshold figure in the emergence of novelistic character. One way to interpret the first line of the play, Bernardo's "Who's there? (I, i) is to see it as the opening salvo in a series of questions preoccupied with human identity.

We can also take the relation between Hamlet and the Ghost of his father (King Hamlet) as an allegory of the novel waiting in the wings of the drama for its moment to appear. The ghost, who enters the play bearing the authority of a traditional, even stock character, gives Hamlet the motive and warrant to act the revenger, a conspicuous moral and dramatic type. His directives, however, have the effect of stranding his son on the threshold where his "flat" if charismatic character as a revenger begins to curve toward the round. We can see the curve taking shape in Hamlet's notorious indecision about staying *in* the dramatic role assigned to him. The wavering, melancholy, and half-suicidal disposition revealed in his soliloquies is totally unsuited to the public and filial duty character his father has commanded him to discharge.

We get another, more interior glimpse of the proto-novelistic nature of Hamlet's predicament in an emotionally charged exchange with his mother that comes early in the play. Gertrude is worried by her son's protracted grief and the erratic and despondent behavior that seems to follow from it. She urges him to accept the consolation offered by the thought that death is "common" to all, and asks "why seems it so particular to thee?":

> Seems, madam? Nay, it is. I know not "seems."
> Nor customary suits of solemn black,
> Nor windy suspiration of forced breath,
> No, nor the fruitful river in the eye,
> Nor the dejected havior of the visage,
> Together with all forms, moods, shapes of grief,
> That can denote me truly. These indeed seem,
> 'For they are actions that a man might play,
> But I have that within which passes show;
> These but the trappings and the suits of woe.
> (I, ii, ll. 76–86)

The problem for Hamlet is that he has no way to give an expressive shape to what is within him, no form, as he puts it, to denote him truly. It is a problem exacerbated by grief, but not confined to it.

To find, and if need be, to invent this "true" form is the great project of the novel. This project is announced and is already well underway the moment Don Quixote, putting on the trappings of knight-errantry, declares when challenged: "I know who I am." We will soon examine how creditable his claim to self-knowledge actually is, but there is little reason to doubt that Don Quixote, unlike Hamlet, feels he has found the form that denotes him truly – it is a form of chivalric existence that he has resurrected and specifically adapted to his own particular, spiritually bereft condition. Hamlet has neither the powers nor the generic license for such self-invention. Hence the melancholy of the Dane, trapped on the stage and in a genre that cannot satisfy his need for a form that "can denote [him] truly" in all that is, as Gertrude says, "particular" to him.

It is this need that is satisfied by the novel, which can accommodate, as no other literary genre can, what is particular to individual character. Not just accommodate, but welcome. This willingness to greet the most surprising characters is exemplified by Ralph Touchett, a character who acts as both an interested spectator and a delegate of the reader in Henry James's *The Portrait of a Lady*. We know we are to trust Ralph's personal view of Isabel Archer, the "lady" who is the novelistic subject of James's portrait, by his reaction upon being introduced to her by his mother: "You've never surprised me but once," he tells (or teases) her, "and that's today – in presenting me with a pretty cousin whose existence I never suspected." Ralph goes on to explain that it is not her prettiness but "her general air of being someone in particular that strikes me." This strikes me as indicative of the way the novel thinks about its characters, especially those marked out as heroes and heroines – they are distinguished by their air of being someone in particular. What these particulars *are* becomes of immense and absorbing interest, as confirmed in the rush of questions Ralph proceeds to ask about the surprising being who has just come into his life: "Who is this rare creature, and what is she? Where did you find her, and how did you make her acquaintance?"[17] Who and what is she, where does she come from, how do we get to know her – these are the questions that provide the novel with its narrative motive and its energy for discovery. They are questions that can only be answered in concrete rather than in general or abstract terms: they demand information about the particular setting and circumstances, the relevant social as well as personal facts that might explain how a character became or will become, not just anyone, a flat and disposable counter, but a someone in particular with a definite life and singular destiny of her own.

Ralph's excited and imaginative response to Isabel represents, of course, the ideal case. Gilbert Osmond, the man Isabel, to her misfortune and somewhat to her discredit, will marry, asks very different questions about her: "Is she beautiful, clever, rich, splendid, and universally intelligent and unprecedentedly virtuous: It's only on those conditions that I care to make her acquaintance" (PL, p.291). Here is a fine example of that "genial crudity" (PL, p.290) that so distinguishes Osmond's character, a defining trait he tries to conceal behind the aristocratic aloofness affected by the arriviste, egomaniacal monster he truly is. We might remember this the next time we demand that *all* our heroines be beautiful, clever, rich, splendid, and universally intelligent before we deign to make their acquaintance.

James's fine discrimination between the different ways we respond to and value characters – either as Ralph does, for their general air of being someone in particular, or as Osmond does, by focusing only on those attributes of the most socially exalted and moneyed kind – finds unlikely and quite hilarious confirmation in *Murphy*, Beckett's mordant satire on the very notion of what it means to have or to love a character. Murphy, the title character, is first shown sitting naked in his rocking chair, secured by seven scarves that help appease his body so "that he could come alive in mind, as described in section six." (Readers are encouraged to drop this book instantly and consult section six.) But Murphy, alas, does have a body, which impels him toward Celia, who has a protector and pimp, Mr Kelly, who subjects Celia to a series of impertinent interrogations: "Who is this Murphy," he cried, "for whom you have been neglecting your work, as I presume? What is he? Where does he come from? What is his family? What does he do? Has he any money? Has he prospects? Has he any retrospects? Is he, has he, anything at all?" Here are all the questions that, if answered, would banish the surprise and solve the mystery of character: the who, the what, and the where to, as well as the where from (its prospects and retrospects), of character; its how and how come, its being and its doing. Celia, overwhelmed by this barrage, takes the first point first and gives a reply that dispenses, without answering, the rest: "Murphy was Murphy."[18]

That he is. A Centrality. An Undisplaceable Force that would prefer not to be translated into the novelistic register of "demented particulars." The true form of character is not to be found in the prose forms of officialdom – the birth and death certificates, the catalog of traits and *curriculum vitae* inventorying actual, but often misleading accomplishments. As Emerson suggests, character is more like "an acrostic or Alexandrian stanza – read it forward, backward, or across, it still spells the same thing."[19] But this Emersonian insight into the tautology and self-sufficingness of all real character, that it is what it is, that Murphy is Murphy, is too abstract for our immediate needs and requirements as readers of novelistic character. Yes, Murphy was Murphy, just as Robinson Crusoe is Robinson Crusoe, but that is the beginning, not the end of our inquiries. To see what makes character something other than the sum of its particulars, we need a vocabulary for identifying what I have called the genus to which such inimitable characters nonetheless belong. One of the purposes of this book is to develop such a vocabulary, to give novelistic characters not only a name, but a "class" of their own.

Novel Types

This may strike some critics and readers as quixotic at best. James Wood has ventured, for example, that "there is no such thing as 'novelistic character.'" Rather, Wood not inaccurately remarks, there are "just thousands of different kinds of peoples, some round, some flat, some deep, some caricatures, some realistically evoked, some brushed in with the lightest of strokes."[20] Of course the differences among characters runs into the thousands, but that is to approach them from outside. It is enough to make us throw our hands up in despair at the mere thought of trying to sort through them all to detect any family or generic resemblances.

But we don't need to sort through them all by ourselves. We have at our disposal a rich and moreover a surprisingly supple vocabulary for talking about different kinds of characters. Amelia Rorty, for example, very usefully and vigorously contends that "heroes, characters, protagonists, actors, agents, persons, souls, selves, figures, individuals are all distinguishable. Each inhabits a different space in fiction and in society." She suggests a way of discriminating them as follows:

> Characters are delineated: their traits are sketched; they are not presumed to be strictly unified. They appear in novels by Dickens, not those by Kafka. Figures appear in cautionary tales, exemplary novels and hagiography. They present narratives of types of lives to be imitated. Selves are possessors of their properties. Individuals are centers of integrity; their rights are inalienable. Presences are descendants of souls; they are evoked rather than represented, to be found in novels by Dostoevsky, not those by Jane Austen.[21]

This is how an accomplished philosopher gifted with literary sensibility sets about discriminating among the different kinds of "persons" our language, literature, and experience recognize.

I admire these distinctions and will depend upon them. But I propose to use terms that novelists themselves have adapted from the usages, moral urgencies, and psychological vocabulary of their day. I propose a somewhat different and radically simplified taxonomy of novelistic characters organized around the following terms: Originals; Individuals; Selves; Identities. They are terms that are more loosely, but also more fully, suggestive of the different psychological and moral constitution of novelistic characters. While they are not terms exclusive to any historical period, they do have their particular "linguistic" moment of cultural ascendancy: talk of Originals, like claims for originality, is more prevalent, as we might expect, in the first novels and becomes rarer as we approach the present day, where characters have all they can do to ward off the socializing designs of collectivist ideologies, identity politics, and tribal or ethnic factions. Individuals rise to prominence during the nineteenth-century, emboldened by the spread of democratic and economic doctrines that fostered the ideal of self-development. The characters of much twentieth-century fiction struggle to attain the unity and be accorded the dignity enjoyed by Individuals; they feel themselves split up into separate, often contending Selves or Identities (sexual, racial, ethnic, or national) that represent only one among the many parts of the integrated whole they would like to be, but seldom are. The fiction of the new millennium, born out of the waning of identity politics and transformations in the world order, envisions the emergence of the Native Cosmopolitan, a new character whose adaptive traits and behaviors suggest their cultural provenance and predicament as migratory or displaced peoples. I do not offer these terms as rigid categories into which novelistic characters can be conveniently slotted. Their value consists in providing a vocabulary at once specific, yet flexible enough to reflect the subtle but important differences in the way the novel has represented human character over time.

For there is no question that novelistic characters represent a new order of literary being that has no settled generic or human form and that is evolving even as I write. Unlike their ancestors in epic and romance narratives, novelistic characters can neither boast of divine progenitors nor count on the favor – or enmity – of the gods. They make their way through the world unattended by wizards, necromancers, nature spirits, or any other creatures with supernatural powers. They are the natives of a fictional genre devoted to exhibiting life, as Samuel Johnson remarks in Rambler 4, "in its 'true state,' diversified only by accidents that daily happen in the world, and influenced by passions and qualities which are really to be found in conversing with mankind." Johnson doesn't put "true state" in quotation marks, as I have felt compelled to do, so confident is he that he knows exactly what is "really to be found in conversing with mankind."[22]

Let us not question, much less attack this confidence, but benefit from the insights it yields us about the relation between certain genres and the characters who bring them to life. None of the genres that preceded the appearance of the novel are terribly worried about representing life in its "true state." Epic magnifies and broadens, romance colors and embellishes, drama concentrates and intensifies the Life they represent. The novel is, as Virginia Woolf called it, a cannibal[23] that feasts on all these genres, so hungry is it for the greatness, the fantasy, the cathartic dramatic exaltation that eludes us in ordinary, everyday life. But it is precisely the everyday life that the novel, as Johnson insisted, takes as its central subject. The life represented in the novel is only accidentally or dimly glimpsed in the epic and romance world of gods, men, and monsters, a world in which life was depicted primarily in terms of its perilous, not ordinary moments. The heroes of epic and romance are distinguished by their extraordinary courage and cunning, the heroines by their beauty and moral delicacy. Unlike ordinary mortals, their fates are overseen and often jealously decided by Olympian gods or an active and not just a watchful Providence.

Milan Kundera emphasizes that this "removal of gods from the world" constitutes "one of the phenomena that characterize the Modern Era."[24] The novel is born out of this crisis in spiritual authority. It rushed in to occupy the spiritual space vacated by the disappearing gods and delivered it over to History; it took upon itself the task, which it regarded as a vocation, of recording modernity in all its living immediacy. It is out of this demythologized landscape that the Originals of the novel emerge. They incarnate the novel's vision of human nature in its highest form.

Endnotes

1 Ralph Waldo Emerson, "Character," *Essays: First and Second Series* (New York: Library of America, 1990), p. 273.

2 R. C. Jebb's 1870 translation of *The Characters of Theophrastus* can be found online at http://www.eudaemonist.com/biblion/characters.

3 Charles Dickens, *Great Expectations* (New York: Penguin, 1996), p. 123. Hereafter GE.

4 George Eliot, *Middlemarch* (Oxford: Oxford World Classics, 1998), p. 140. Hereafter M.

5 John Stuart Mill, *On Liberty* (Oxford: Oxford University Press, 2008), p. 67.

6 Mill, 2008, p. 66.
7 Emerson, 1990, p. 265.
8 Nadine Gordimer, *Writing and Being* (Cambridge: Harvard University Press, 1995), p. 15.
9 Gordimer, 1995, pp. 2–3.
10 Gordimer, 1995, pp. 2–3.
11 Gordimer, 1995, p. 15.
12 Sigmund Freud, "Creative Writers and Day Dreaming", *The Complete Psychological Works of Sigmund Freud* (New York: W. W. Norton, 1976), Vol. 9, pp. 143–53. Hereafter SE (Standard Edition).
13 Georg Lukács, "Thoughts on an Aesthetics of Cinema" (1913), *German Essays on Film*, ed. Richard W. McCormick and Alison Guenther-Pal (New York: Continuum, 2004), p. 14.
14 E. M. Forster, *Aspects of the Novel* (New York: Harcourt Brace and World, 1954), pp. 103–4.
15 Forster, 1954, p. 105
16 Forster, 1954, p. 118.
17 Henry James, *The Portrait of a Lady* (New York: Penguin, 1986), p. 96. Hereafter PL.
18 Samuel Beckett, *Murphy* (New York: Grove, 1957), p. 17.
19 Emerson, 1990, p. 36.
20 James Wood, *How Fiction Works (*New York: Farrar, Strauss and Giroux, 2008*)*, p. 106.
21 Amelia O. Rorty, "A Literary Postscript: Characters, Persons, Selves, Individuals", *The Identity of Persons* (Berkeley: University of California Press, 1976), p. 302.
22 Samuel Johnson, "Rambler 4," *Samuel Johnson: The Major Works* (New York: Oxford University Press, 2008), p. 175.
23 Virginia Woolf, "The Narrow Bridge of Art", *Collected Essays*, ed. Leonard Woolf (London: Chatto and Windus, 1967), Vol. 3, p. 323.
24 Milan Kundera, *Testaments Betrayed* (New York: Harper Perennial, 1992), p. 8.

I

Wholes

2

Originals

Originals are by definition the first of their kind, but not all firstcomers are Originals. Herman Melville, who recognized Original characters when he encountered – and created – them, was jealous of their reputation and eager to preserve their integrity. In *The Confidence Man*, his deeply unsettling satire on human guile and its ready victims, he takes time off from his narrative to consider what human qualities we are honoring when we describe someone as "quite an original." Melville is so irritated by our casual way with this compliment to human ingenuity that he devotes an entire, albeit short chapter of *The Confidence Man* to correcting our undiscriminating conceptions of Original character. He complains that the phrase is "rather oftener used by the young, or the unlearned, or the untraveled, than by the old, or the well-read, or the man who has made the grand tour." "Certainly," he insists, "the sense of originality exists at its highest in an infant, and probably at its lowest in him who has completed the circles of the sciences."[1] Undoubtedly. Originality may not be as common as the young and unlearned believe, yet their conviction represents, as Emerson passionately argued, "claims not to be put by."[2]

The novel at once upholds and investigates the validity of those claims. As the "infant" in the family of epic and prose narratives, the novel is eager to see and seek out originality in the unique ways human beings make their presence felt in the world. It is fascinated by the varieties, vagaries, and occasional splendor of human character, no matter how flawed or imperfect, even somewhat deranged (witness the first novelistic hero and Original, Don Quixote). But the novel is also the renegade offspring of Renaissance humanism, which expanded "the circle of the sciences" to include the empirical study of human character. Precisely because the novel esteems Original characters, it is determined to present the most objective picture possible of what makes originality so hard to come by and once achieved, preserved. This is one reason why the novel is host to a variety of human types, but very few Originals.

Melville appreciated how rare genuine Originals were and indeed suggests that only literature gives us reliable sightings of them. He acknowledged and greeted them in the characters of Hamlet, Don Quixote, and Milton's Satan, the latter the precursor and model for his own daimonic hero, Captain Ahab. He was careful to distinguish Original characters from their rivals or foils who act in a "singular, captivating or entrancing manner" rather than with self-authenticating Force. The difference between the two was stark, at least to Melville's novelistic eye: "While characters merely singular imply but singular forms, so to speak, original ones, truly so, imply original instincts" (CM, p.205). The singular character expresses his or her singularity in the personal form in which, Melville contends, it is exhausted. The Original Man or Woman (a possibility Melville does not seem to have considered, but whose moral reality preoccupied Flaubert in creating Madame Bovary, Thomas Hardy in his bewitched vision of Eustacia Vye as a Queen of the Night, Tolstoy in loving and lamenting the noble but baffled soul of Anna Karenina) is a premonition of new instincts in humanity. Originals, we might say, are the first and sole speakers of a new language of Being germinating within them. It is for this reason that Melville thought the Original character should be recognized as a great prodigy "as in real history is a new law-giver, a revolutionizing philosopher, or the founder of a new religion" (CM, p.205).

Of course counterfeit Originals abound in literature, as they do, alas, all too frequently in life. Melville offers us a way to distinguish them. "There is discernible something prevailingly local, or of the age," he observes, in the pretenders to Originality. What is "deemed original" in them "is but something personal – confined to itself." What is original to the Original cannot be confined, but, like Don Quixote's madness, spreads and spills over into reality, transforming everything in its wake. Nor can the Original be reduced to a category or be enlisted as a representative of class, race, gender, ethnicity, or any "local" accidents of birth. Original characters do not epitomize the prevailing sentiments and established values of their historical moment, but heed the promptings of seminal Instincts that often have no tangible objects in the world as it is. Thus an Original like Don Quixote feels compelled to "restore" the appearances of the ordinary world through which he travels to their original forms as enchanting and enchanted objects. Melville conveys the Original's transformative presence and powers in a striking image. He likens the Original to "a revolving Drummond light, raying away from itself all round it – everything is lit by it, everything starts up to it (mark how it is with Hamlet), so that, in certain minds, there follows upon the adequate conception of such a character, an effect, in its way, akin to that which in Genesis attends upon the beginning of things" (CM, p.205).

Melville's homage to Original characters presiding over the beginning of things echoes Emerson's conception of Character as "a reserve force which acts directly by presence, and without means," but in a concrete image that theatricalizes it. The Drummond light is a fixture of the stage, a limelight, to use its more common name, that illuminates the central presence and highlights the decisive action of the drama being played out before and, as it were, beneath it. It is a light that isolates and illuminates in the same irradiating movement. This image is suggestive, then; it attributes to Original Character a radiant power that resembles the form-giving light of Genesis. The light cast by the Original Character is a form-seeking light, a luminescence associated with the beginning of things, the start, as it were, of a new scene or act in the human pageant. What follows from that beginning is, in many ways, the subject of this book.

Quixote: Or the Originality of Imitators

Originals, then, are identified with luminous beginnings. A light emanates from them that, when turned onto the world, discloses unsuspected dimensions and new possibilities within and beyond the existing order of things. But Originals also cast a fresh light on the Past in the very act of leaving or transforming it. They have a double consciousness of Time in which the Future is twinned with its Origin in an idealized or Lost Past. They are aware, in ways more ordinary and less clairvoyant characters are not, of the numinous as well as obscurantist presence of Tradition. In Don Quixote, the novel's first and greatest Original, this double consciousness takes the form of a lucid, even cunning madness. For Don Quijano, a man of La Mancha of otherwise sober and regular habits, the Past exists as a rich and endlessly entertaining archive of fabulous romances and epic exploits. He devotes so much time to pondering their mysterious meanings and imaginative audacities that he loses his wits. But that hardly begins to describe what is happening within him. Those hours spent with his beloved books of chivalry prove to be the seedtime for new instincts whose flowering transforms his sense of what life is *for*. When these new instincts, as instincts inevitably do, assert themselves, Don Quijano loses "his sense of reality" – a phrase any lover of fiction and Originals should treat with suspicion. He refuses to identify his true Life with the scarcities and uneventfulness that have marked his everyday existence and retreats – or rather advances – into a fantasy world where all the excitements and rewards imaged in fabulous fictions – the exalted love, the eternal fame, and the promise of endless as well as ennobling adventure – await him. We are closer to the spirit of Originals if we say that in losing his sense of ordinary reality, Don Quijano gains the moral clarity of the more exalted and purposeful existence of Don Quixote, a (self-created) knight-errant dedicated to reviving the historically extinct, but morally vital tradition of chivalry.

The very word Original, in its modern as well as traditional sense, would seem to support the rightness of his Instinct. It derives from the Latin *origi*, to rise, a meaning and heritage also preserved and elaborated in the word for "orient." An origin is the source from which new life arises and around which we, creatures of light, orient ourselves. This original sense of the radicalness (another "root" word) of the Original inheres in Don Quixote's madness; it transfigures his madness into a form of prophecy in which the new world of the novel is not just foretold but announced as already here, indeed as having been around us all along. His madness does not jeopardize, but validates, admittedly in its most extreme form, the paradoxical character of novelistic Originals – their origin, the source from which they arise like a new daystar, is as much behind as before them. They lead us towards the future, orienting themselves by the light of the Past that often shines only within them.

This paradox engenders another, one that Melville does not consider when he distinguishes Originals from the throng of "singular" characters that threaten to dim, steal, or eclipse the strange light emanating from them: the dutifulness the Original feels toward his or her Self-Origin, or, more accurately, toward the myth of Origins to which he or she subscribes. The instinctive piety of novelistic Originals complicates as much as it validates their status as Originators. Emerson taught that there comes a time in our moral education when we "arrive at the conviction … that imitation is suicide."[3] One of the things that marks the novel as an infant, or let us say, less prejudicially, a *young* form, is its reluctance to reach that conclusion. The Original character of its first hero, Don Quixote, is rooted in the child's love of Imitation. And like a child, Don Quixote is not afraid to be an imitator, so secure is he in the answering force of his own nature, which Imitation can shape but never deform or distort. On the contrary, he feels fulfilled in imitating his revered model, Amadís of Gaul, just as later Stendhal's Julien Sorel, that genius in imitative camouflage, elevates and empowers himself in identifying with that world-historical upstart, Napoleon. What distinguishes such Originals is their imaginative and passionate choice of models that others, whether of singular or conventional character, dismiss as old-fashioned, unrealistic, impracticable, too demanding, or outright insane.

Don Quixote is never deterred by such fears and admonitions. However much he is mocked and despite the many mortifying falls, beatings, and humiliations he endures, he never falters in pursuing his sacred mission as a Faithful Follower of the Venerable Order of Knight-Errantry. It is a duty he owes to himself as much as to the righteous warriors with whom he identifies. "I know who I am,"[4] Quixote famously, indeed irritably proclaims after his first, somewhat ignominious fall, annoyed that he can be questioned about something so obvious to himself. But what exactly is it that he knows about himself? Evidently that it does not matter what his "real history" or given name might be. With astounding nonchalance, he dismisses such facts as "of no importance ... since each man is the child of his deeds" (DQ, p.37). In fact, he doesn't give his name, only the assurance that he knows who he is. That assurance seems based on the understanding, peculiar to himself, that the more perfectly his actions imitate those of his models, the more secure will be his place in the Tradition with which he so devoutly and insanely identifies.

The problem always before him is not *whether* to imitate, but *who* or *what* to imitate. The ingenuity that the novel's title – *El ingenioso hidalgo don Quijote de la Mancha* – identifies as his signature character trait is exemplified in his decision to imitate the melancholia of Amadís rather than the madness of Roland in performing his erotic penance in the Sierra Morena: "Long live the memory of Amadís," he cries, "and let him be imitated in every way possible by Don Quixote de la Mancha, about whom it will be said, as it was said of the other, that if he did not achieve great things, he died in the effort to perform them ..." (DQ, p.206). In such moments, René Girard claims, "Don Quixote has surrendered to Amadís the individual's fundamental prerogative: he no longer chooses the objects of his own desire – Amadís must choose for him." Amadís thus represents a particular kind of model, that of the "mediator," as Girard identifies him, who occupies the apex of a triangle at whose base we find the desiring subject (Quixote) and the desired object (chivalric existence).[5]

Girard's claim that Quixote is a "victim of triangular desires" strikes me as a just and irrefutable one. Yet there are some forms of victimizations that are heroic, that impress us as unlikely, but undeniable spiritual triumphs. In the passage Girard quotes to open his marvelous book, Quixote does indeed submit to the authority of Amadís, but on specific terms. For one thing, he does not pretend that his actions are spontaneous, and in fact becomes anxious that they conform to the exact letter as well as general spirit of the Code of Knight-Errantry, a Code he has committed to memory precisely to ensure that his Imitations will be as spiritually effective as they are aesthetically correct. His actions as knight-errant, however absurd, are not the erratic improvisations of a madman, but the ritualized performances of an Original. For another, he declares that Originality is the goal, not the antithesis of his Imitations, and even cites established artistic practices in defense of this belief, observing that "when a painter wishes to win fame in his art, he attempts to copy the original works of the most talented painters he knows"(DQ, p.193). He regards his own acts of Imitation as a form of aesthetic as well as moral discipline that, if followed to the letter (a crucial condition), will transform him, a decrepit hidalgo fallen on hard times, into a hero for the ages. Imitation, as Don Quixote understands and embraces it, is the discipline to which all aspiring creators must submit, even if, indeed especially if, the object to be created is not a painting or a sculpture but one's own self. Seen in this light, his Imitations appear, at least to me, as pragmatic as they are comically absurd. Moreover, he knows that his chosen model, Amadís, is "one of the most perfect knights errant" in the same way that Ulysses is a model of carefulness and patience or Aeneas of valor and piety, exemplary figures who are depicted "not as they were but as they should have been"(DQ, p.193).

The "ideal" character whom Don Quixote imitates in order to secure his own originality is described in the same imagery of light that Melville associated with the "true" Original: Amadís, Quixote asserts in a figure that anticipates Melville's trope, "was the polestar, the morning star, the sun to valiant and enamored knights." A polestar, morning star, a sun, a Drummond light – all are figures of the radiant, at times blinding Light from which new things emanate or are made visible. Thus while it is true that Don Quixote's duty toward himself is indistinguishable from his piety toward his Model and Source-Tradition, it is also true that this piety takes the form of an imitation so ingenious that it creates an unprecedented and surprisingly contagious way of seeing and living in the world: the Quixotic.

Common usage now dismisses the Quixotic as the signature trait of ineffectual dreamers forever tilting at windmills. We lose much by settling for this conventional, careworn meaning. We lose, for one thing, a sense of the volatile power that may be unleashed against the disenchanted and disenchanting world. Tilting at windmills is but one of the ways in which Don Quixote presumes to subjugate commonplace reality to a more exalted vision of what the world might be. This is the gist of all his efforts to educate his loyal but temperamentally pragmatic squire, Sancho Panza, about the actual and ideal (as opposed to the apparent) nature of the world. Sancho, to invoke Melville's distinction, is a singular, but hardly Original character who habitually views reality through the lens of common sense, relying on proverbs and folklore to interpret what he sees.

Don Quixote takes great pains to show Sancho the limits of this way of seeing things. Those who take the appearances of the world as real, he repeatedly warns Sancho, have been blinded to the splendor of reality by fiendish enchanters who fool us into thinking that things can never be other than what they seem to be. "Everything," he tells Sancho, "is artifice and mere appearance, devised by the evil magicians who pursue me … as proof of this you already know, O Sancho, through experience that will not allow you to lie or deceive, how easy it is for enchanters to transform one face into another, making the beautiful ugly and the ugly beautiful" (DQ, p.195). In such moments, Don Quixote is almost literally a lunatic who sees the world as if by moonlight rather than in the light of common day. His lunatic eye detects evidence that enchanters of every description and persuasion are invisibly and relentlessly at work disguising the true nature of the world and of the people and things within it. But with the reasonableness that uncovers the profound moral sanity lurking within his madness, Quixote, the Original, caps his argument by appealing to the authority of experience, which proverbially "cannot lie or deceive." This is an argument Sancho is likely to understand and accept.

If the appeal to experience strikes us present-day moderns as preposterous and comical, that is because we have not yet succumbed, as Sancho, the reader's most trustworthy delegate in these matters, already has, to the authority of the Original's way of looking at things. This, indeed, is one of the most important services Sancho provides in the novel – to question his Master's logic, even his sanity, but ultimately to subscribe to the Quixotic version of how things really are and how they can one day be. He speaks not only with the authority of common experience, but in its most enduring voice – the language of proverbs and the commonplace idioms of everyday life. But as many critics have noted, most wittily the Spanish critic Salvador de Madariaga in speaking of the "quixotification of Sancho Panza," Sancho is also the first victim of the Quixotic contagion, leaving his wife and family to accompany a man who instead of offering to pay him for his services, promises something more valuable and, seemingly, out of reach: an "insula" of his own. In Sancho's gradual quixotification the novel is not so much questioning the limits of common sense and proverbial wisdom as expanding the number of things experience might include.

That is genuine as well as honorable work for Originals. In the novelistic regime inaugurated and ingeniously defended by Don Quixote, experience is not limited to material facts, like a person's name, income, social status, diet, family, and friends. Experience encompasses the immaterial but nonetheless authentic realities to be found in books; it includes the urgencies of spiritual as well as physical needs and can accommodate the most intense, delicate or erratic motions of the mind. "Nature and books belong to the eyes that see them," wrote Emerson in a strikingly quixotic passage from his own essay on "Experience."

Such is the Credo of Originals. It is a Credo whose imperatives are not, however, always encouraging or benign in their consequences. Faith may justify a man, but it can also enrage him at those who doubt what he believes. Don Quijano is described as a man of regular habits and discreet appetites with a fondness for the hunt. After his transformation into Don Quixote, knight-errant, his behavior becomes more intemperate; there are times when he seems genuinely "furioso" – the heroic epithet of one of his models, the romance hero Orlando. This intemperance is obvious from his very first sally. Meeting a band of merchants from Toledo who appear to him to be knight-errants, he demands that they halt in their tracks and "confess that in the entire world there is no damsel more beauteous than the empress of La Mancha, the peerless Dulcinea of Toboso" (DQ, p.39). The cleverest among them engages Don Quixote on his own logical (if absurdist) ground, promising that he and his companions will happily do so if they could only set eyes on this paragon of female grace.

But Don Quixote's reasoning is superior to any argument that appeals to common rather than Original experience: "If I were to show her to you," he counters, "where would be the virtue in confessing so obvious a truth. The significance lies in not seeing her and believing, confessing, affirming, swearing, and defending that truth ..."(DQ, p.39). Faith is the evidence of things not seen, a precept Quixote interprets in an original fashion, that is, in a way that is at once orthodox (faithful to origins) and heretical (with its root sense of "choosing" a meaning for oneself). As his challenge to the skeptical merchants demonstrates, his faith is founded on an obvious, but generative error: confusing things unseen with things that are imagined. This error is compounded by another, more serious one: Quixote's faith here is at its most militant, compelling others to believe as he believes. He is a man on a quest, but he is also a man looking for a fight. Sometimes these urges are hard to tell apart.

The novel, however, is the book of errant, not permanently settled or morally impeccable characters, so we can expect such confusions whenever we try to "read" a character's motives or assess the moral nature and quality of his acts. The inevitability of such confusions redoubles the obligation of novelists to resist taking the part of their Original characters, however much they may be tempted to do so. Cervantes' novel is exemplary in this regard, and in fact derives its plot, its humor, and its rare but genuine moments of pathos from episodes that put Don Quixote's faith to the test. Throughout his adventures, Don Quixote is constantly coming across those whose dull or roguish or merely beleaguered eyes look upon Nature and the Human World through the shuttered lens of convention. Initially this contradiction between Don Quixote's perceptions and what the rest of the novel's characters protest is the patently visible truth of things forms the basis of the simple, if wonderfully variable formula in which his imaginative vision of things collides with things as they are all too plainly – and commonly – seen. But this comic formula, ideally suited to dramatize the perennial opposition (an opposition that often escalates to open and sometimes brutal hostility) between appearance and "reality," a word, Nabokov reminds us (and who should know better?) should always be used in quotations marks, could yield only so many variations, ingenious and entertaining as they might be, on Cervantes' heretical theme. As Don Quixote travels deeper into the world of contemporary, modern Spain, the comic formula yields to a more complicated equation that factors other ways in which Reality can, indeed *must*, be reckoned with.

The acquisition of Sancho Panza as his squire is the first term in this new reckoning with Reality. His employment (unpaid) is mandated by the rules of knight-errantry, but Sancho's entry into the novel comes in the service of a subtler campaign against the endemic injustices and common, but genuine evils of modern life. If we briefly retrace the initial arc of Quixote's adventures once he has secured Sancho as his squire, we can see their comic exploits increasingly expose them to the harsh and often pitiless order of things. Here is the sequence of episodes that mark out the spiritual itinerary of Quixote's quest:

SHEEP → CORPSE → FULLING MILLS → MAMBRINO'S HELMET → SLAVES

The arc of his travels, which recapitulates the movement of the novel from idealized reveries to the most fettered realism, takes him from the pastoral to the picaresque, from a herd of sheep he mistakes for an army of infidels to a gang of criminals condemned to work as galley slaves. The sheep are hallucinated images of the chivalric age behind him, the galley slaves of the modernity, with its iron laws, before him. Huddled between are the experiences that will reveal the kind of Originality possible to an Imitative Genius.

At first this genius seems of a low, if entertaining order. Don Quixote's mistaking a herd of sheep for an army of infidels is, after all, a novel variation on the dependable formula that pits his exalted vision against a mundane and in this instance amusingly placid reality. But his next encounter with a caravan transporting a corpse for burial relocates such comic misperceptions in the territory of the uncanny. Don Quixote and Sancho are riding along a lonely path on a dark night when they glimpse on the black horizon "a great multitude of lights that looked like nothing so much as traveling stars"(DQ, p.135). Sancho fears that an adventure with phantoms is upon them, while Quixote, despite his own apprehensions, welcomes the prospect of demonstrating his courage against what he believes to be a troupe of demons from hell. These glittering nocturnal lights, which shimmer on the horizon like traveling stars, suggest how Don Quixote's character gravitates not only toward the Origin but also toward the End of all things, of which the corpse is a natural emblem. Its lifelessness stands for the final victory of the reality principle over the pleasure principle, whose highest and most impossible quixotic desire is a Life of endless adventures, that is, a Life in which Death is perpetually postponed or outwitted. Quixote instinctively responds by attempting to "liberate" the corpse from the desecration Death has inflicted upon it.

This instinct will come to define him. For it is after this phantasmagoric encounter with death (later Death will appear personified as a figure in a puppet show) that Don Quixote acquires the epithet that will henceforth distinguish him as the Original figure he so unmistakably is. The name is given to him by Sancho Panza, who in this, as in so many future episodes, shows himself to have the most subtle as well as most complete knowledge of his master's spiritual character: El Caballero de la Triste Figures, the Knight of the Sorrowful Face as his most recent translator renders it, but elsewhere and memorably translated by the English novelist Tobias Smollett as The Knight of the Rueful Countenance, a rendering I prefer for its slightly antiquated diction, which seems to me more befitting an Original who is also an anachronism. Don Quixote may pattern his melancholy after his adopted model, Amadís, but its spiritual causes are to be found in his own experiences with the body of death and in his Original responses to them.[7]

This Quixote of the "triste figura" is the knight of faith whom the Spanish philosopher and Quixotephile Miguel de Unamuno hailed as "Our Lord," a spiritual leader "whose madness makes us sane."[8] Unamuno considers Quixote's madness spiritually therapeutic and, indeed, redemptive, because it only emerged and flourished "after his sanity and goodness were well-seasoned." "He was never a lad," writes Unamuno, "who threw himself helter skelter into an unfamiliar career, but a judicious man who went mad from pure maturity of spirit."[9] An Original begets original notions: here Unamuno identifies an Original form of madness, one that matures and fulfills rather than obliterates the sane, established character of those who fall victim to it. This is a view that Don Quixote takes of his own transformation from a decent man of reduced estate into a morally grandiloquent hero. When, at the conclusion of the second sally, he is conversing with the canon on the questionable morality of chivalric romances, many of which had been burned as offensive to God and to common sense at the conclusion of his first sally, he defends them by citing the spiritual reformation they have worked in his own nature:

> For myself, I can say that since I became a knight errant I have been valiant, well-mannered, liberal, polite, generous, courteous, bold,

> gentle, patient, long-suffering in labors, imprisonments, and enchantments, and although only a short while ago I saw myself locked in a cage like a madman, I think that with the valor of my arm, and heaven favoring me, and fortune not opposing me, in a few days I shall find myself the king of some kingdom where I can display the gratitude and liberality of my heart. For by my faith, Señor, the poor man is incapable of displaying the virtue of liberality with anyone, even if he possess it to the greatest degree, and gratitude that consists of nothing more than desire is a dead thing, as faith without works is dead. (DQ, p.430)

Harold Bloom wonders what the true object of Don Quixote's quest might be and concludes that, like the question of Hamlet's motives, it remains an enigma that is probably unanswerable.[10] Perhaps. But we are concerned here with Origins and Originators and how they see themselves; in this instance we are particularly concerned with a privileged moment in which Don Quixote's moral lucidity and his madness reinforce rather than oppose or undermine each other. At such moments, the object of his quest looms conspicuously visible not so much before as within him: moral beauty.

We should not mistake or dismiss this vision as a narcissistic mirage. Quite the opposite is the case. His Original instincts, as Melville might say, are not confined to himself. His vision of the moral beauty he has attained, while lit from within, encompasses and is generously identified with social, other-directed virtues: a warrior's physical courage and moral valor; a knight's courtesy towards those he serves; patience in adversity. We can appreciate the moral grandeur of Don Quixote's self-conception by comparing it to Sancho's hilariously venal definition of a knight-errant: "someone who's beaten and then finds himself emperor"(DQ, p.110). Sancho efficiently reduces the romance of knight-errantry into a brisk tale of self-enrichment. But Don Quixote doesn't desire to be King, but to be kingly. He longs for the means and seeks the opportunities to display the liberality of spirit teeming within him. In his madness, he may never correctly "see" the nature of the people and objects that attract his attention, but there is something generous in his mistaking wenches and whores for ladies, or idly grazing sheep for marauding armies who threaten the people and land he has sworn, if only to himself, to defend.

Quixote's magnanimity toward the fallen world of appearances recalls, but also radically amends the First and most mystifying Beatitude of the Sermon on the Mount – "Blessed are the poor in spirit, for theirs is the kingdom of heaven" (Matthew 5:3). "Blessed are the rich in spirit," Don Quixote seems to be saying in describing his new life as a knight-errant, an inversion of spiritual terms in which irony joins forces with pathos. His need to confirm and distribute his own spiritual riches inspired Don Quijano to cast off his historical identity as a sane, gaunt gentleman who is sustained by lentils, amused by the occasional hunt, and whose only adventures are those encountered in books. He knew or simply felt that as Don Quijano he would always be among the poor in spirit in the way he interpreted that hard and demanding phrase – lacking the means to proclaim and enact his Faith in Deeds. So it is that the impoverishments of reality goad him to ever more ingenious and unrepentant follies.

Original Claims and Final Reckonings

But the spiritual rewards of folly may be greater than those of wisdom, as Paul advised in his First Letter to the Corinthians and Carlos Fuentes, in a more secular spirit, remarks in describing *Don Quixote* as "a Spanish extension of the praise of Folly."[11] Quixote's foolishness is at once exposed and vindicated in his memorable encounter with a barber whose basin he takes to be that chivalric relic, Mambrino's Helmet. A dispute understandably results over what the basin really is and how much, if anything, it is really worth. This dispute is the most momentous in Quixote's career, since its outcome will determine the legitimacy of the Quixotic regime of novelistic experience.

What makes this particular adventure so exceptional is that it is one of the rare occasions when Don Quixote actually sees the basin as it appears to ordinary eyes as well as it appears to his own,

Original ones. He does not, as he usually does, summarily dismiss Sancho's protest that things are what they appear to be, but instead speculates on how the helmet was splintered and degraded into a barber's basin:

> This famous piece of the enchanted helmet, by some strange accident, must have fallen into the hands of one who could not recognize or estimate its value, and not knowing what he was doing, and seeing that it was made of purest gold, he must have melted down one half to take advantage of its high price, and from the other half he made this, which resembles a barber's basin, as you say. Be that as it may, I recognize it, and its transmutation does not matter to me. (DQ, p.155)

It is the particular misfortune of Mambrino's Helmet to be divided into two, one half whose value is determined by the price it will bring, the other by the use to which it is put. What was once (and Quixote believes still is) a chivalric icon has been degraded into a commodity, a degradation that indicates, as no other episode yet has, the split character of novelistic reality. Quixote is for the first time confronting the double as well as disenchanted nature of things. This knowledge does not, as we might expect, disconcert or enrage him. Rather he finds further vindication of his Original talent for recognizing things in their "true state," attributing the blindness of others to the "rare foresight of the wise man who favors me to make what is really and truly the helmet of Mambrino seem a basin to everyone else, because it is held in such high esteem that everyone would pursue me in order to take it from me" (DQ, p.195).

Nonetheless, the bright things of this world are not so easily possessed; they must be paid for in the hard, if glittering coin of the realm. At the close of the first part of his adventures, the claims and counter-claims about the reality and worth of Mambrino's Helmet/the barber's basin are literally put to a vote. That the reality of things can be established by consensus is a novel proposition in every sense of the word, but one whose meaning and implications are by no means clear, much less sanguine. We note that only those with rank and power are enfranchised to vote. The Quixotic Original sees and recognizes things for what they "truly and really are." Those in power do not so much see as *determine* what things are, a subtle but monumentally important difference. Moreover, with the characteristic indifference of Power to poverty, those who decide on the fate of the basin neglect to reimburse the barber for an object as vital to his livelihood as the Helmet was to Mambrino and, presumably, to Don Quixote in the performance of his chivalric duties. It remains to the priest attending the proceedings to secretly pay the barber for the loss of his basin. Why a priest and not the noblemen who presume to decide on all questions of property? Perhaps because only a priest would remember and feel obliged to act on Christ's injunction, "Render unto Caesar the things that are Caesar's."

The world is split: how to divide it? Jesus gives one answer. Quixote, all too human, devises another solution, but even he comes to understand that his way of seeing the world must be paid for. The price tag attached to novelistic experience is what distinguishes it from those epics and romances in which, as Don Quixote initially remarks, make no mention of wages, bills, payments for food, shelter, and all the necessities as well as conveniences of life. Don Quixote, who does not know that the barber has been compensated, discovers this harsh fact for and within himself when, on his third and final sally, he descends into the cave of Montesinos. There he falls into a waking dream in which the legendary figures of chivalry coexist and intermingle with his own mad creations, the most Original being Dulcinea, whom he is shocked and grieved to discover stripped of her finery and reduced to begging half a dozen *reales* from her loyal knight. "Is it possible," he asks the wizard Montesinos, "that distinguished persons who are enchanted suffer from need?" (DQ, p.612) This being a dream-vision, we may take Montesinos to be ventriloquizing Don Quixote's innermost conviction that Need infuses all forms and levels of existence when he answers that "what is called need is found everywhere, and extends to all places, and reaches everyone …"(DQ, p.613).

Money is one way of satisfying Need, of ransoming Life from the poverty that threatens to despoil, degrade, and even extinguish it. From its inception the novel acknowledges Money as one of the Lords of Experience. *Don Quixote*, for all its fancifulness, exhibits a precise grasp of the fluctuating values of goods and experiences. Dulcinea, even in her enchanted state, requires not some reales, but half a dozen reales. Yet if Money can solve our material wants, it does not answer to the needs of the spirit. Render unto Caesar what is Caesar's, but, adds and insists the Quixotic Original, render to the spirit what the spirit values. And what does Don Quixote value? Above all, he values Images, Models to imitate. His days as a knight-errant come to end not when he runs out of money or exhausts the patience of those willing to underwrite his fantastical escapades, but when he comes to the end of those Images that alone signify and sanctify Life for him. Which is exactly what happens when he and Sancho come upon a group of farmers transporting wooden images of saints destined to adorn the altar in their village. Each image, the villagers proudly tell him, cost fifty *ducados*, but that is only what they cost, not what they are worth. Their value for Don Quixote can only be reckoned by their power to ignite his own desire to "display the gratitude and liberality in my heart."

These images, the last he will encounter, are also the most sublime: St George, St Martin (pointedly described as "another Christian seeker after adventures"), and St James the Moor killer. The last and most exalted image is of St Paul, depicted at the moment of his conversion in so lifelike a manner that "one would say that Christ was speaking and Paul responding." These images of militant faith appear, then, like a valediction. Don Quixote's quest for enhanced and ennobled life reaches here a culmination that fulfills but also exhausts his Source-Tradition. The moment, while spiritually climactic, comes with little fanfare: Don Quixote looks around to see if he might behold other figures worthy of his esteem and imitation, but finds, as the narrator quietly reports, that "there were no more images" (DQ, p.834).

How could there be? In St George, St Martin, St James the Moorkiller, and St Paul, Don Quixote contemplates Knights of

Faith in their most sanctified form. Without any more images to exalt him, he is cast back upon himself. Unable to project himself heavenward, Don Quixote suddenly loses sight of, and then faith in, his Original labors:

> Brothers, I take it as a good omen that I have seen what I have seen here, because these saints and knights professed what I profess, which is the practice of arms; the difference, however, between me and them is that they were saints and fought in the divine manner, and I am a sinner and fight in the human manner. They conquered heaven by force of arms, for 'the kingdom of heaven suffereth violence,' but so far I do not know what I am conquering by the force of my labors ... (DQ, p.834)

Although Don Quixote proclaims what he sees to be a good omen, Unamuno detects in this avowal, rightly I think, the voice of "disheartenment" that reveal Don Quixote's "spiritual brotherhood" not with saintly knights of old, but with "the mystics of his own Castilian land." Unamuno hears in these words "the lament of a soul at finding itself alone."[12]

Don Quixote's isolation is of a particular kind, however. In actuality, he is hardly left a moment to himself. Sancho will never desert or betray him. Some of the (imagined) readers of Book I become characters who pursue, mimic, and entrap him (sometimes literally) in Book II. In the course of his adventures he converses and consorts with wenches, goatherds, muleteers and convicts, innkeepers, tradesmen and itinerant entertainers, distracted or runaway lovers from every social class, priests, warriors, judges, landowners, and even a duke and duchess. At novel's end he returns home to a family and to neighbors who remember him as much for his goodness as for his mad exploits. Don Quixote ends his life not wanting company, but bereft of those Images of knightly valor and liberality that were his spirit's true companions. He is the first of the novel's great spiritual castaways, attempting to put together a new world out of the wreckage of the old.[13] Robinson Crusoe, the Original of the English novel, is the second.

The English Original

That Robinson Crusoe should turn out to be such an Original is as much a wonder as any of his adventures on and off his island, given how much of the "local," as Melville might say, went into the making of his character. His pragmatic temperament and habits of mind speak of a character representative, as James Joyce proposed, of "the whole Anglo-Saxon spirit: the manly independence; the unconscious cruelty; the persistence; the slow yet efficient intelligence; the sexual apathy; the practical, well-balanced religiousness; the calculating taciturnity." Yet Joyce appreciated that Defoe was creating more than a national archetype in attributing these characteristically "English" traits to Crusoe. In his view, Defoe was "the first English author to write without imitating or adapting foreign works, to create without literary models and to infuse into the creatures of his pen a truly national spirit, and manufacture an artistic form which is perhaps without precedent (except for the brief monographs of Sallust and Plutarch) ..."[14] Joyce proclaims Defoe the "father of the English novel" (and thus his own progenitor) and Crusoe is his most original creation.

But in what does his Originality consist and from what new and profound instinct does it spring? In the wanderlust that compels him to leave home, despite the prudential middle-class advice of his father to seek and remain in the middle station of Life where fortune and adversity are least likely to seek him out? In the empirical and entrepreneurial spirit that emerges, in a new moral flowering, once he lands on an uninhabited island that tests the limits of his ingenuity in creating a world answering to his immediate and future needs? In the instinct to find or make tools that will maximize the return on his labors? In the pragmatic spirituality that reckons, as he notoriously does, the blessings and banes of his existence as so many items in a ledger whose sum total promises to solve the riddle of Salvation? In the long-deferred but immediately gratified instinct for mastery once he rescues Friday and makes him his first island subject, a premonition, as Joyce believed, of the character of British imperial rule?

Around this uncanny human figure, clothed, like a latter-day shaman in his animal skins, armed with an umbrella to shield him from the sun, shadows continue to accumulate. They dog his steps as he moves, with increasing confidence, into the sun-drenched landscapes of myth.

This aura of myth that slowly forms around the plain facts of his narration is one reason for Crusoe's enduring life in our tradition. Another is that his luster has been enhanced by the proximity of other Originals. For Originals can attract other Originals, a phenomenon something on the order of a double-star. Jean Jacques Rousseau's admiration for the islanded Crusoe is one such phenomenon. Rousseau regarded *Robinson Crusoe* as the "best treatise on natural education" ever written and made it the central text in the moral training of his literary child, Emile. Crusoe occupies the same revered place in Rousseau's revolutionary course of moral development as Amadís in Don Quixote's self-perfecting Imitations. In the noble, but delicate and often miscarried work of human formation, Crusoe was the lodestar to help us find our way: "The surest way to raise oneself above prejudice and to order one's judgments on the true relations of things is to put oneself in the place of a solitary man and to judge all things as they would be judged by such a man in relation to their own utility."[15] Through this imaginative exercise, Rousseau hopes that Emile should come "to know things that are useful, and only the things that are useful." Rousseau's proposed method for learning the true value of everything is one of the first and most consequential flowerings of Crusoe's original "island" instincts.

This view is confirmed by another Original, Karl Marx, who, with a somewhat different sense of play, offered the islanded Crusoe as the incarnation of *homo economicus* in his pure state:

> … our friend Robinson … having rescued a watch, ledger, pen, and ink from the wreck … commences as a true-born Englishman, to keep a book about himself. His inventory contains a list of useful objects that belong to him, of the operations necessary for their production, and (lastly) of the labour-time that given quantities of

> those different products tend to cost him. All the relations between Robinson and the things which form his wealth he has himself created are so simple and perspicuous as to be intelligible without special exertion ... And yet these relations contain all that is essential to the determination of value.[16]

"Our Robinson" proves, however, to be more complex than the simple and perspicuous Laborer Marx depicts. Joyce, for example, saw the seeds of colonialist rule in Crusoe's pragmatic and administrative genius, but there are other elements in his character that portend a new instinct for solitude and the sultanic dreams that are encouraged by a solitude so complete. He fancies and indeed promotes himself as a landowner (albeit for an economy of one) and something of an island plutocrat. The longer he stays on the island, the more his judgment of value is warped by a grandiosity dormant until awakened by his uncontested dominion over the island. The Rousseaustic paragon who protests in one passage that the "Nature and Experience of Things" have taught him "that all the good things of this world, are no farther good to us, than they are for our use" is the same man who later grandly refers to his country house and his sea-coast house as island "estates" which he admits to surveying "with a secret Kind of Pleasure."[17] Even if we allow, with Emerson, that character wants room, Crusoe provides himself with more square footage than is necessary to secure shelter from a pitiless sun and violent storms. Pleasure, not well-reasoned appreciation for the utility of things, begins to infiltrate his "true" relationship to objects, especially the things he has built or built up with his own hands.

This pleasure in imprinting his distinctive mark – or character – on the things that constitute the material foundation of his existence becomes less secret and more immodest, if not shameful, as the years go by. The commoner advertised in the title as a mariner of York is not above comparing himself to sitting kings, as he does when, surveying his island properties, he thrills to the thought that "this was all my own, that I was King and Lord of all this Country indefeasibly, and had a Right of Possession; and if I could convey it, I might have it in Inheritance, as compleately as any Lord of a Mannor in *England*" (RC, p.73).

How self-aware or ironic Crusoe is in entertaining these waking dreams of kingly sovereignty is hard to determine. The question would be easier to answer if Crusoe were not so disinclined to mull over morally delicate matters relating to his own instincts and desires. Crusoe takes to the sea because, among other things, it offers him a chance to avoid the self-evaluative habits of his father's Puritan creed. Once stranded on his island, things prove no different. This strikes me as a remarkable fact about his character. Surely no character in English fiction has ever been given more time, with less distractions, for self-study than Crusoe and no character has seemed less inclined to use it for that express purpose. Still, the amount of time devoted to searching for the truth about oneself is no guarantee of results, as anyone who has tried it can tell you. Crusoe, not a habitually, much less constitutionally reflective character, nonetheless does confess to relying on what he calls his Intuitions, what we may generally call instincts, to enlighten him as to the nature and disposition of his own character. They prove to be disturbingly original. This is what they tell him:

> But I was born to be my own Destroyer. (RC, p.31)

He at first means something quite obvious, even superficial and conventional by this. He may even be offering it as a moral alibi for the restlessness that leads him to dismiss his father's advice to secure and profit from a place in the "Middle Station or upper Degree of low Life" where harm and misfortune are unlikely to find him, and to reject any form of employment "remote to my Genius and directly contrary to the Life I delighted in ..." (RC, p.27). Crusoe considers his own Genius to be as a seeker after pleasure, which explains, at least to his own mind, his flight from the prudential, self-moderating manners of the stay-at-home middle class into which he was born. Although not the expert casuist and "indifferent monitor" of his own actions that Moll Flanders is, Crusoe, whose cunning is instinctual rather than intellectual, is quick to attribute his errant ways to the self-undermining will that is, he believes, the chief legacy of the Fall:

> I have been in all my Circumstances a *Memento* to those who are touched with the general Plague of Mankind whence, for ought I know, one half of their Miseries flow; I mean, that of not being satisfied with the Station wherein God and Nature has plac'd them; for not to look back upon my primitive Condition, and the excellent Advice of my Father, the opposition to which, was, *as I may call it*, my ORIGINAL SIN. (RC, pp. 140–41)

The first thing to be noted about Crusoe's conception of original sin is how original it is. As a point of orthodox doctrine, Original sin refers to the sin of Adam and Eve, the cause of the Fall and the origin of Death, a mortal punishment passed on to all succeeding generations of humankind. Original sin is not something we commit, but a mortal taint we inherit at birth. In this disarming bit of heterodoxy, Crusoe acknowledges his social character as a rebellious and prodigal son, while insinuating that he represents, in fact, a distinct spiritual type. Hence his claim that "all my circumstances" declare him to be a living "Memento" of restless genius, unwilling to accept things as they are and seem destined to be.[18]

Crusoe is both a Memento and a Prophecy of restless instincts that have yet to find a settled human or social form. The very genius that makes Crusoe his own destroyer compels him to obey those very instincts – secret Intimations of Providence, he calls them – which will make him into an Original. Like many an Original, Crusoe's instincts often take the form of premonitions that foresee the very conditions in which they can be gratified. Such, at least, seems to be case of the curiously prescient thoughts that plague him while working away on his plantation in Brazil:

> But alas! For me to do wrong that never did right, was no great Wonder; I had no Remedy but to go on; I was gotten into an Employment quite remote to my Genius, and directly contrary to the Life I delighted in, and for which I forsook my Father's House, and

> broke thro' all his good Advice ... In this manner I used to look upon my Condition with the utmost Regret. I had no body to converse with but now and then this Neighbour; no Work to be done, but by the Labour of my Hands; and I used to say, I liv'd just like a Man cast away upon some desolate Island, that had no body there but himself. (RC, p.27)

Here is where I begin to suspect Crusoe of coyness, or, worse yet, of artfulness. Such artfulness would cast a shadow over his reputation for candor, since Crusoe, unlike Moll and Roxana, Defoe's equally if differently resourceful female narrators, is not a particularly untrustworthy narrator of his own life. Nonetheless, when he claims that he "used to say" that he lived just like a man cast away on some desolate Island, is he telling us that he was unconsciously prophesizing the ironic course of events that will turn a figure of speech into the actual "Condition" of his existence? Or is he expressing, which is equally plausible, a secret and persistent wish of finding himself on an island where the self-destroyer in him might finally emerge in its true and naked – that is, in its Original – form?

The feeling that some self-fulfilling prophecy of imperious instinct is the secret author of Crusoe's castaway adventures finds its most uncanny and comically bathetic expression in the "bemoaning" Voice that rouses him from his work-wearied sleep with a series of direct, almost accusatory questions: "*Robin, Robin, Robin Crusoe,* poor *Robin Crusoe,* where are you *Robin Crusoe?* Where are you? Where have you been?" "But judge you, if you can," Crusoe challenges us, "what a Surpize I must be in, when I was wak'd out of my Sleep by a Voice calling me by my name several times"(RC, p.104). The Voice, we soon discover, is that of his beloved parrot, Poll. Here Crusoe gives us a logical and perfectly "natural" explanation for the Voice that accosts him. Of course this explanation no sooner solves the mystery than it discloses a deeper one concerning the hidden springs of Crusoe's vagabond character. Surprise in these circumstances is all the more wondrous for being a form of self-surprise. For surely the bodiless Voice is his own, ventriloquized by Poll, whose repeated catchphrases memorialize Crusoe's island ordeals.

The parrot, we might say, is keeping an anniversary of the day that Crusoe encountered himself as an Original.

This episode suggests that Crusoe, contrary to the evidence of his journal, in which he enters the barest facts of his existence, is, in fact, developing an awakening narrative interest in the course of his own life. One of the questions he teaches Poll to repeat is "How came you here" – the narrative question par excellence. Michael Seidel has demonstrated how subtly these questions dramatize the peculiar doubleness of exilic life in which where you are and where you have been, the homeland and exilic land, become fused and superimposed upon each other.[19] These questions, moreover, are variations on the original questions that puzzle and plague all actively self-inquiring human consciousness: how came we to be where and who we are. These are questions about our origins. While we may dodge them if we so choose, they are inescapable questions for an Original.

That the supreme adventure for Crusoe in exile involves his confrontation with the mystery of origins is dramatized in the two "miracles" that testify to the Original Destiny that at once isolates and exalts him. One we might call the parable of the seeds, in which Crusoe discovers rice and barley sprouting where none had ever grown before. His first response is to believe "that God had miraculously caused this grain to grow without any help of seed sown, and this was so directed purely for my sustenance in that wild miserable place." But once he recalls that he had shaken out a bag of grain to feed chickens on that very ground "the Wonder began to cease; and I must confess my religious Thankfulness to God's Providence began to abate too upon the Discovering that all this was nothing but what was common" (RC, p.58). Crusoe's determination that "all this was nothing but what was common" is in keeping with the novel's general inclination to seek the natural rather than supernatural causes for the strange things that can and do happen to us. But the problem with logical explanations is that they can fail to distinguish material causes from spiritual effects. Crusoe appears to us more in his character as an Original when he treats the sprouting seeds as signs of the special dispensations made for him in the divine scheme of things.

However self-centered this interpretation may be, it has the virtue of acknowledging and honoring the mystery of generative processes, including those germinating within his own character.

The other miracle, less explicable and more consequential for Crusoe's moral understanding of the precariousness of his islanded life, is the appearance, never explained, of a single footprint in the sand. Crusoe is unnerved by the sight, almost as if he had suddenly found himself, the quintessential Empirical Man, thrust *into* a parable, whose meaning eludes and therefore frightens him. He begins to "tremble at the very Apprehensions of seeing a Man," and confesses himself on the verge of sinking "into the Ground at but the Shadow or Silent Appearance of a Man's having set his Foot in the Island" (RC, pp. 113–14). Crusoe will spend the next two years speculating on who might have made that print (he initially fears it might have been Satan amusing himself by taking on human form to enjoy a stroll on a beach where no one might spot him!) and fortifying his defenses. But even in his final and more reasonable conjecture that the footprint was made by "savages" from the mainland who had been blown off course, he sees a special providence acting to preserve him. So arresting is Crusoe's description of the physical fear the mere sight of that footprint aroused in him that it is easy to overlook the almost casual way he reports that it was from this time that he began to call his island home his castle. Hardly the instinct of the natural man nor of the spiritually cowed and repentant one. But it is the instinct of an Original reinforcing, if only psychologically, his claims to kingly sovereignty over his territories and over himself. Years pass and nothing happens to dislodge this fixed idea of himself. By the time he rescues Friday and inducts him into his service, he has reached the point where he insists on being called Master not as a social or linguistic convenience but in formal recognition of his Supremacy. Hence the hint of threat in Crusoe's reporting that he taught Friday "to say *Master*, and then let him know, that was to be my Name" (RC, p.149).

Self-naming is one of the prerogatives of novelistic originals – Don Quijano takes full advantage of that opportunity to commemorate the beginning of his new life as a knight-errant. Walter Shandy had hoped to launch his son into life by christening him Trimesgestus, thrice blessed, believing that such an auspicious name might serve his heir as an amulet against disaster, but, alas, his son is christened Tristram, the very name (with the obvious exception of Judas) he had expressly declared as a harbinger of misfortune and obliquity. Crusoe is noteworthy in the early annals of the novel for his unexplained, but clearly strategic desire to be addressed by his (self-appointed) title rather than by his proper (or assumed) name. Crusoe will not teach Friday what he took such pains to teach his pet parrot – how to say his name. In this, too, he shows himself in his "character" of self-destroyer, for in giving up his name, he is also relinquishing his highly developed and idiosyncratic private character to a more generic public role. He thus ensures that there will be only one direction for the self to expand – outwardly – and one form that expansion can take: self-aggrandizement.

Self-aggrandizement, not self-ennoblement, which was the spiritual motive of Don Quijano's giving birth to an ideal self who answers to the name of Don Quixote. Island life has summoned Crusoe's instinct for mastery from the inner recesses where it lurked, awaiting the providential conditions that would permit it to sprout as extravagantly as those miraculous seeds of grain. Once it begins germinating, this instinct becomes surprisingly prolific in creating fantasy roles that might satisfy Crusoe's increasingly magnificent sense of himself. All of them are, indeed, quite grand: Crusoe likening himself to a Giant, which appeals to the primordial being within him; Crusoe flattering himself as a veritable king over his island domains. His instinct to rule is satisfied in his professedly benign but complete subjection of Friday and his successful conscription of the marauding, mutinous sailors who later invade his island into his newly constituted army over which he, as self-appointed Generalissimo, exercises absolute authority.

There is something childish in these dreams of precedence – to see oneself, however deprecatingly, as a giant, to consider oneself undisputed master in one's society (if only a society of two), to assume the rank, along with the uncontested authority, of a generalissimo. Such fantasies are nurtured by island life, but they do not necessarily expire there. They are assimilated into a new pride in being an Original. Crusoe ends his island exile by leading a double campaign to subdue the invaders and arrange for the end of his island captivity. In setting out, he reports that the troop he has assembled "did me the Honour to call me Captain, as well because I was the oldest Man, as because I had two servants, and indeed was the Original of the whole Journey" (RC, p.208).

Let us not overlook either the importance or the presumption of this claim just because it is reported with relatively little fanfare. Where his troop honors him with the title and authority of Captain, Crusoe assumes the mantle of the Original, as if it were his due. Which it is. He survived the very calamities that he, a self-proclaimed self-destroyer, had unconsciously courted and succeeded in fashioning for himself not just a new, but a more imperious character, a regal personage whose most frequent and "merry Reflection" is "how like a King I look'd." It is an Original reflection, to say the least, that concentrates all the preciously scattered Force of his character into an image of himself as the "absolute Law and Lawgiver" (RC, p.174) with "Right of Dominion" over his property, his subjects (few, but obedient) and himself.

A madman with a savior complex and a Castaway who would be King – these two unlikely figures of eccentric ambition are the great Originals of the novel. They forged paths that others, as Crusoe says, are bound to follow. They were seekers after Experience who, though born in different countries, times and cultures, possessed of different temperaments and driven by different spiritual and physical needs, survived, through the original force of their character and their magnificent vision of who they might be, the moral isolation that lies at the heart and in the way of all genuine human adventures.

Conversations with an Original

Quixote had immediate imitators, both within the novel chronicling his adventures and in the novels that succeeded him, a lineage that extends from and unites Fielding's picaresque, spiritually more hapless heroes and Charlotte Lennox's *Female Quixote* to Salman Rushdie's *The Moor's Last Sigh*. But the seeds germinating in Crusoe remain relatively dormant until their more lavish flowering in later ages, most notably in Joyce's exilic fictions and in the spiritual disaster narratives of Muriel Spark (*Robinson*), J. M. Coetzee (*Foe*), and the emigrant narratives of V. S. Naipaul, in which the cultural and existential shipwrecks of the postwar, postcolonial world of the mid- to late twentieth century are recounted with comic grimness. Crusoe's solitariness took such an original form that the novel could not immediately pursue his methodical, but strangely lyrical tracks into a solitude so complete, so troubling, and ultimately so transfiguring. Crusoe alone on his island was unable, both by virtue of his circumstances and his character, to fulfill the novel's generic mandate to show, as Samuel Johnson described it, "passions and qualities which are really to be found in conversing with mankind."

Originals may or may not be the most accomplished Conversationalists, but their inviolable, surprising, and instinctively restless character changes the scope of that conversation and the way it is conducted. Even the briefest glance at the foundational works inaugurating the reign of novelistic Originals confirms that the fledgling novel, eager to expand its conversation with mankind, began to show a marked proclivity for chronicling the adventures, lives, and opinions of gregarious rather than self-isolating characters. Robinson Crusoe, whose first and most memorable narrative of adventures was published in 1719, and Samuel Richardson's Clarissa, whose tragic ordeals were made known in 1748, are Originals as distinct in class, experience, and temperament as it is possible for heroes and heroines to be, but they are alike in this one decisive particular: they only become Originals in isolation and captivity. The solitary cast of their lives is succeeded and countered by the more sociable fictions of Fielding and Sterne. The strange moral glare of Crusoe profiled against the pitiless island sun, or the luminous force of Clarissa, the sole illuminant among the dark devisers who ensnare and imprison her, are replaced by less resplendent, but cheerier figures of Life. Fielding's *Tom Jones*, appearing in 1749 a year after the final volume of *Clarissa*, presents us with a physically splendid and morally heartier hero. Ten years later the world is graced with the first installments of *Tristram Shandy*, whose life and opinions cast a warmer, if melancholic light on the oddities of human character.

Both Fielding and Sterne conduct their conversations in the genial mode of their model and mentor, Cervantes. But both entertain radically different ideas about how and indeed whether to disassociate Quixotic force of character from the underlying madness that fuels and sustains it. Fielding is the more gregarious and loquacious recorder of this conversation in all its various registers, from the vigorous rustic idioms of country squires and the communities that serve and surround their estates, to the most elegant and treacherous patois of London salons. Sterne is the more skeptical that the conversation really is a conversation, and not just an opportunity to voice, a capella, the singular melodies coursing through our minds.

Fielding, a novelist who Johnson thought never approached Richardson as a chronicler of human passions, nonetheless subscribed to the same aesthetic tenet, insisting that the novelist's conversations with mankind constitute "another sort of knowledge beyond the power of learning to bestow." The sort of knowledge that matters to Fielding is knowledge of characters; hence his prominence in this history, however abbreviated and idiosyncratic, of novelistic character, even though, as we shall see, he created no fictional character who could be called an Original or could be said to have had a conversation with himself. Fielding is as concerned with moral beauty as Cervantes, but his sense of goodness is not encumbered with the psychological burden of originality. *Tom Jones*, arguably the most socially as well as geographically expansive novel of its time, is filled with eccentric, lovable, vile, loathsome, petty, self-interested, duplicitous, lecherous, ill-tempered, mean-spirited, and good-hearted characters, as entertaining a company as one might hope to meet within the pages of a book. But not one of these lively creatures unsettles the genial, but lordly narrator who never will or could be surprised by anything his characters are and do.

Take the case of Mrs Wilkins, a minor character who gives Fielding's narrator a chance to show how low as well as high, wide, and deep his conversation with mankind extends: "It is my intention, therefore to signify that, as it is the nature of a kite to devour little birds, so it is the nature of such persons as Mrs Wilkins to tyrannize over little people."[20] The narrator assures us that he can be so sure of Mrs Wilkins's nature, because hers is a part, a consistent and knowable part, of human nature: "We do not pretend to introduce an infallible character into this history, where we hope nothing will be found which hath never yet been seen in human nature" (TJ, p.117). Now if we are in search of Originals, the narrator's hope will dash our own. We will be disheartened by the assurance that we will never encounter a character "which hath never been seen in human nature." Fielding's novelistic world is inhabited by characters who, however idiosyncratic, singular, or eccentric, confirm our experience of human nature, rather than unsettle and expand it.

This being so, *Tom Jones* is in danger of turning its more attentive and morally scrupulous readers into scholastics too busy parsing the Book of Nature to pursue any reported, but unauthenticated sightings of Original creatures scampering across its pages. Fielding is more concerned to ensure the integrity of his translations than in creating Original characters who promise to rewrite the Book of Nature or at the least add their own singular testimony to it. No loose translations are allowed in Fielding's Book of Human Nature, either; no contradiction or inconsistencies in behavior can go unexplained, no sudden mood swings or changes of heart occur but they can be rationally accounted for. There is nothing, or very little, in Fielding's rendering of character to suggest how ultimately mysterious, strange, and opaque human beings can be. He in fact assures his readers that he has taken great care to ensure that his characters' actions

> should be such as may not only be within the compass of human agency, and which human agents may probably be supposed to do; but they should be likely for the very actors and characters themselves to have performed; for what may be only wonderful surprising in one man, may become improbable, or indeed impossible, when related of another.

> This last requisite is what the dramatic critics call conservation of character and it requires a very extraordinary degree of judgment, and a most exact knowledge of human nature. (TJ, p.351)

We can see the advantages, but also the limitations in the conservation of character as a novelistic, as opposed to strictly dramatic, device for representing human behavior in Fielding's morally generous, erotically game, and self-baffling hero, Tom Jones. Fielding's scapegrace protagonist occupies the transitional space few characters are brave or foolish enough to enter – a kind of no-man's land between singular and original character. His affability and good humor never develop into an original instinct. Not the genius but the good "nature" and virility of the race is incarnated in him. That good nature and virility might be at odds with each other in certain erotically charged and compromising instances is a possibility that threatens to move the novel into murkier territories than Fielding's sunny hero is accustomed to and would probably not survive if marooned there for any length of time. But of course he is not marooned there. The novel only threatens to abandon him in the mire, darkness, and opacity of myth in raising the specter of an Oedipal encounter with his mother. Tom is providentially spared the ordeals of Oedipus in discovering the scandal of his own origins and confronting human nature in the form of a riddle.

What Tom must resolve is less an Oedipal riddle than an Oedipal quandary, one that places and suspends him between the two male polestars of the novel: Allworthy, the Lord of Paradise Hall, a character whose name and manner/manor identify him as an Edenic figure of Fatherhood; and Squire Western, who is violently insistent on his own mindless will. The figures align themselves almost too conveniently with Freudian agencies within the self: Allworthy, figure for the Super-Ego, the internalized voice of the father, the voice of moral restraint "striving for perfection" and condemning thoughtless, offensive, immodest, and importunate desires; Western, his name suggesting a direction rather than a value, a figure of the

Id, reckless, always in pursuit of pleasure, but also procreative (as Allworthy – sadly or curiously, even notoriously? – is not). Both professional critics and lay readers have been drawn to Western's character as the more vital and amusing. We enjoy, almost to the point of indecency, Squire Western's reprobate company (what reader, no matter how sophisticated, doesn't impatiently wait, after Western departs the scene, for the next time he will burst on the scene, all bluster and force?) even if we might be morally alarmed at the thought (never seriously entertained) that he will make good on his threats against the daughter he adores.

If we are ultimately more amused than appalled by Western's rants and threats against his daughter, it is because we trust Fielding's comic authority and skill in containing whatever aberrant energies Western releases into the novel. More troubling to me than Western's anarchic vitality is the moral presumption advertised in the name of Allworthy, precisely because there does not seem to be any comic corrective attempt to penetrate the haze of benign motives through which Allworthy acts and moves. His name identifies him as a paragon of charitable and rational behavior, an identification that the novel confirms in describing him as "a human being replete with benevolence, meditating in what manner he might render himself most acceptable to his Creator, by doing most good to his creatures" (TJ, p.37). This is as morally commendable a life as one can imagine. Yet there is something limited and limiting in Allworthy's benevolence, since it imaginatively and emotionally restricts the active scope of his moral will. He can never wander far from himself, act out of character (both the allowances he makes for Tom and his banishment of him from Paradise Hall comport with his idea of himself as a fair as well as judicious man). Allworthy never has nor does he seek the opportunity to investigate the principle that symbolically defines and limits him.

Thus it seems to me worth asking what, in fact, is the principle and measure of human worthiness that Allworthy incarnates. To put it another way, what makes a character worthy of all things: esteem, fortune, happiness, all the moral goods in life that will eventually come Tom's way? This is not a question that is likely to come up on a deserted island where, assuming one survives, one can call one's time, one's life, indeed the very ground one stands on one's own. Tom's worthiness is comically allied to the question of what it is to be, or to look like – an angel:

> Indeed he was a charming figure; and if a very fine person, and a most comely set of features, adorned with youth, health, strength, freshness, spirit and good nature, can make a man resemble an angel, he certainly had that resemblance. (TJ, p.428)

Luckily for us, that is, luckily for the novel, Tom may resemble, but he decidedly doesn't act like an angel. His name alone translates him decisively – and safely – out of the precincts of angelic life into the ranks of healthy, fresh, spirited, handsome, but distinctly ordinary creatures who must find their own moral way to beatified existence – which, in secular terms, translates into a life full of blessings. That is the great moral task of the genuine Original – the quest for foundational principles for a new order of life. In this regard, Tom's lack of curiosity toward his own Origins and his unquestioning acceptance of the benignity as well as rightness of Allworthy's judgments alone would disqualify him from the ranks of those self-seeking, self-authenticating characters who represent the true Originals of the novel. On the other hand his character makes as good an argument as we have for the value of instinctive vitality over original instincts.

This liveliness is what the picaresque form offers in place of Original characters who make their own values. Fielding's expansive and hospitable imagination seized upon the wide geographical and social latitudes encompassed by the picaresque, which allowed him to take his characters (worthy and unworthy unlike) on the road, in search of happiness but never really in quest of themselves. But their very mobility, as Martin Price observed, contains the suggestion of a spiritual movement that prepares the way for Originals to come:

> Picaresque heroes are necessary whenever we wish to celebrate those virtues than cannot be – or simply haven't been – embodied in our

> morality. These heroes may be socially mobile men in an age of outgrown establishments, or they may be champions of values that society, by its very organization, necessarily represses. The resilience and survival of the picaresque hero is a survival of the values he stands for, values too closely involved with action to be put to sleep in Avalon. They must be seen in their readiness and their openness, and the picaresque work often concludes with the arc of a new gesture to be made.[21]

The new gesture is made with singular, extravagant, and endearing wit in *Tristram Shandy*, a novel whose hero recounts, more as a family legend rather than personal history, the ordeal of his own begetting and birth. In fact, we might say that the novel's interest in origins – its own as well as that of its characters – culminates in *Tristram Shandy*. Sterne's novel is the first great English character study that distills the force of "Cervantick" moral goodness into humors. These humors define and animate the singularly British variation on the theme of Original Being – the eccentric in whom instinct becomes Whim and is sublimated into sensibility.

Sterne's symbol for this nativist, whimsical Humor is the Hobby-Horse, a symbol that is also his solution to the problem of how to draw Original characters. This problem is the comic preoccupation of *Tristram Shandy*, itself a satire on the presumption of rendering any character in the fullness of his life and opinions. Worrying that his readers "must be out of all patience for my uncle Toby's character," he recommends that "there is no instrument so fit to draw such a thing with, as that which I have pitch'd upon."

> A man and his HOBBY-HORSE, tho' I cannot say that they act and re-act exactly after the same manner in which the soul and body do upon each other, yet, doubtless, there is a communication between them of some kind; and my opinion rather is, that there is something in it more of the manner of electrified bodies; – and that, by means of the heated parts of the rider, which come immediately into contact with the HOBBY-HORSE – by long journies and much friction, it so happens, that the body of the rider is at

> length fill'd as full of HOBBY-HORSICAL matter as it can hold; so that if you are able to give but a clear description of the nature of the one, you may form a pretty exact notion of the genius and character of the other.[22]

Plato likened the soul to a team of winged horses guided by their charioteer. The novel is earthbound, and its riders, though as noble as Uncle Toby, sit atop less ethereal creatures: Don Quixote on his dilapidated steed, Rocinante; Uncle Toby astride his hobby-horse. One is an Original, the other a singular character, but both spectacles gives us a pretty exact notion of the genius and character of novelistic heroes.

And Now for Our Heroines

Of heroines, we can make no such unabashed claims. With the notable exceptions of Clarissa Harlowe and Madame de Lafayette's Princess of Clèves, the first heroines of the novel are not Originals or originators. They enter the new world of the novel more constrained and encumbered than their male counterparts by social and sexual customs that are, in Melville's phrase, "prevailingly local, or of the age." Heroines must often struggle to *become* characters and not just paragons whose dreary task it is to protect their virtue and bring credit to their sex. Even if they manage to transcend or avoid or, as in the case of Moll Flanders and Roxana, make a mockery of the idea of the heroine as a paragon, they rarely expand or overturn inherited notions of female character.

Heroines distinguish themselves as characters once the novel begins to consider them in the light of individuals. Their achievements in self-development will be chronicled and assessed in the next chapter. But before we take leave of the novel's first Originals, we should honor a female character with a fierce instinct for an Original existence who is not destined, nor does she desire to become, a heroine. She is Marcela, the beautiful orphaned child of a rich farmer who one day, as suddenly and as unaccountably as Don Quixote takes up arms, adopts the dress of a shepherdess and takes refuge in the Sierra Morena, that haven for those, like herself, in flight from the sorrows, impositions, and moral poverty of commonplace reality. Don Quixote was born because Alonso Quijano felt the need to express his kingly and magnanimous spirit. Marcela becomes a shepherdess to preserve what she insists cannot be bartered, cajoled, paid for, or in any way possessed: her own inviolable self. She rejects love and will not consider marriage – the personal and social objective of most novelistic heroines until fairly recent times. She will not allow her radiant being to be eclipsed by marriage; she will not permit any infringement on her freedom to be herself.

What is "herself"? She tells us in a series of startling and aggressively resplendent images:

> I was born free, and in order to live free I choose the solitude of the countryside. The trees of these mountains are my companions, the clear waters of these streams my mirrors; I communicate my thoughts and my beauty to the trees and to the waters. I am a distant fire and a far-off sword. . . .
>
> If I preserve my purity in the company of trees, why should a man want me to lose it if he wants me to keep it in the company of men? As you know, I have wealth of my own and do not desire anyone else's; I am free and do not care to submit to another. I do not love or despise anyone. I do not deceive this one or solicit that one; I do not mock one or amuse myself with another. The honest conversation of the shepherdesses from these hamlets, and tending to my goats, are my entertainment. The limits of my desire are these mountains, and if they go beyond here, it is to contemplate the beauty of heaven and the steps whereby the soul travels to its first home. (DQ, pp. 99–100).

Marcela sees herself as a liminal figure, defiantly poised between the social domain of men, in which women figure primarily, if not exclusively, as objects of courtship and marriage, and the literary domain of the pastoral, in which human desire is delicately balanced against an idealized Nature. Nature, to anticipate Emily Dickinson, another poetic solitary, is her Soul's Society – trees, water, and mountains are all the company she seems to require. Her faith is directed toward the skies, whose beauty leads her thoughts from this world to its first home in the heavens. We might see in Marcela's meditative yearning to return to her first home a regressive fantasy, a yearning to return to infancy, with its life of sensations rather than erotic entanglements.

But if we take, as I urge we do, Marcela's understanding of her own character as an enlightened, rather than self-deluding one, we can appreciate her as the novel's first female Original, trying to live according to the promptings of a *new* instinct that has not yet found a place in the world. Like Quixote, she shelters the archaic images that give her the courage to become and remain an Original. Thus she conceives of her first home, as Plato and as Christian doctrine conceived it, as a spiritual destination, not as Freud later would, as a regressive flight back to the unfocused and unorganized sexuality of childhood. The skies define a horizon that represents for her what Melville calls the beginning, as well as the destined end, of things. This possibility may escape our notice, because Marcela is founding a novelistic culture without an immediate future, which is to say, Marcela is a founding figure for the tradition of the anti-novel. She withdraws from the newly established novelistic regime of social and monetary inter-relatedness, refusing to be bound by the social conventions that decree love and marriage as woman's highest spiritual aspiration and social fate. In choosing to live in the pastoral world of the Sierra Morena, she abandons the looser but still intimate relations forged out of kinship or friendship or communal and national feeling. She will not answer to being a daughter, a beautiful woman adored by men, or a Spaniard in a novel in which all these categories determine the way all the female characters think of themselves.

Marcela is so uncompromising in her Original feelings about herself that she can hardly expect and luckily does not desire to become part of the novelistic world she helps create. Hers, too, represents a negative, if potent form of Originality, since her very existence is a rebuke to the culture that forces her instinct into such sterile if grandiloquent gestures of self-assertion. She will find an unlikely but equally highborn sister in the Princess of Clèves, another heroine whose Originality is allied to her genius for renunciation, and

Clarissa Harlowe, who can only affirm her Original character by refusing offers that are morally repellent to her. We must wait until the heroines of Jane Austen, the Brontës, and George Eliot to encounter heroines who are not so much the victims or passive agents of the marriage plot but transformers, rebels, even, drawing-room generalissimos like Emma Woodhouse, waging campaigns to enlist others, while reserving for themselves the right of conscientious objector, to the cause of marriage. Their battles may take place in quiet corners and in the most hushed surroundings, but, as we shall see, they are nonetheless fighting for their lives – as Individuals.

Endnotes

1 Herman Melville, *The Confidence Man* (New York: Norton, 1971), p. 204. Hereafter CM.
2 Ralph Waldo Emerson, "Self-Reliance," *Essays First and Second Series* (New York: Library of America, 1990), p. 30.
3 Emerson, 1990, p. 30.
4 Miguel de Cervantes, *Don Quixote*, translated by Edith Grossman (New York: Harper Collins, 2003), p. 43. Hereafter DQ.
5 René Girard, *Deceit, Desire and the Novel*, translated by Yvonne Freccero (Baltimore: John Hopkins University Press, 1985), pp. 2–3.
6 Emerson, 1990, p. 243.
7 This is confirmed in the adventure of the fulling mills that immediately follows. It is the first of many "non-adventures" that nonetheless reveal Don Quixote's character and the nature of his vocation. The episode is the first one in which Don Quixote *sees* nothing and encounters no external obstacle to his mad enterprise; he simply spends the night plagued by ominous sounds whose origin and meaning neither he nor Sancho can account for. The effect of fear, as Quixote tells Sancho, is "to cloud the senses and make things appear other than the are" (DQ, p. 129), an acute psychological observation that in this episode has the force and authority of a (melancholy) confession.
8 Miguel de Unamuno, *Our Lord Don Quixote: The Life of Don Quixote and Sancho with Related Essays*, translated by Anthony Kerrigan (Princeton: Princeton University Press, 1967), p. 25.

9 De Unamuno (translated by Anthony Kerrigan), 1967, p. 27.

10 Harold Bloom, "Introduction" *Don Quixote*, p. xxi.

11 Carlos Fuentes, "Introduction," *Don Quixote*, translated by Tobias Smollett (New York: Farrar, Straus, Giroux, 1990), p. xxvi.

12 De Unamuno (translated by Anthony Kerrigan), 1967, p. 249.

13 De Unamuno sees Don Quixote's quest as mirroring the Spanish "invention" of the New World by those "castaways from Spain" like Cortés and Pizarro and Orellana (the first Westerner to navigate the Amazon River and who gave it is name). The conquistadores were, in this view, knight-errants of the sea "the most vigorous of whom came from deep inland, from Extremadura." [De Unamuno (translated by Anthony Kerrigan), 1967, pp. 424–25.]

14 James Joyce, "Realism and Idealism in English Literature," *Occasional, Critical and Political Writings* (New York: Oxford Classics, 2000) p. 164.

15 Jean-Jacques Rousseau, *Emile, ou de l'éducation*, Book 3. Readers can find an English translation paired with the original French text online at http://www.ilt.columbia.edu/pedagogies/rousseau/em_eng_bk3.html. I have modified the English translation slightly to make the sense a bit clearer.

16 Karl Marx, *Capital: A Critique of Political Economy*, Vol. I, translated by Ben Fowkes (New York: Vintage, 1977), p. 140.

17 Daniel Defoe, *Robinson Crusoe* (New York: Norton, 194), p. 73. Hereafter RC. This edition reproduces the spelling and typography of original text and will be cited as such.

18 The OED lists two entries from Defoe under its definition of Original which corroborate my claim that the instinct for original action is associated with the particular *kind* of Original Crusoe embodied. Under the following entry – "extended use (of a person): that is so by birth or nature; born" – we find the following notation: "Originally with allusion to the idea of original sin; later in more general sense." Then come two striking citations to exemplify this meaning in both its general and theological sense:

> **1720** D. DEFOE *Capt. Singleton* 182, I … was … an original Thief, and a Pyrate … by Inclination. **1723** D. DEFOE *Hist. Col. Jack* (ed. 2) 5 He was an original Rogue.

The belief that persons are who they are by birth or nature is, as these selections attest, normally called upon to explain errant, self-evidently, if often amusingly, "bad" rather than necessarily Original characters.

Whatever originality such errant souls possess is possessed by one and all, as a consequence of our common fallen nature. Their sense of Originality is naturalized in the doctrine of Original Sin, which is seen to be energetically at work in the lives of miscreants, rogues, and ne'er-do-wells. It is a doctrine that Crusoe himself, at opportune moments in his own recollections, uses to explain his own plight and the calamities that befall him.

19 Michel Seidel has commented on these questions in his *Exile and the Narrative Imagination* (New Haven: Yale University Press, 1986).

20 Henry Fielding, *Tom Jones* (Oxford: Oxford University Press, 1996) p. 41. Hereafter TJ.

21 Martin Price, "The Subversion of Forms," reprinted in *Henry Fielding's Tom Jones*, ed. Harold Bloom (New York: Chelsea, 1987), p. 41.

22 Laurence Sterne, *The Life and Opinions of Tristram Shandy, Gentleman* (New York: Penguin, 2003), p. 67.

3

Individuals

"Emma Woodhouse, handsome, clever, and rich, with a comfortable home and happy disposition, seemed to unite the best blessings of existence …"[1] So begins Jane Austen's portrait of her most willful, self-complacent, and imaginatively active heroine. This inventory of her personal traits and social assets serves as our formal introduction to an exceptional heroine, but not an Original one. There is, after all, nothing in Emma's established character and current circumstances that indicates the slightest dissatisfaction with her life, much less any intention to change or reinvent it. For most of the novel she hardly gives a thought to her own future, preoccupying herself instead with imagining and scheming to settle the lives of others. Emma may possess the cleverness and arrogance to "arrange everybody's destiny"(E, p.339), but she lacks the incentives and the moral latitudes to create, as Don Quixote and Robinson Crusoe succeeded in doing, a new regime of value.

On the contrary. Everything appears right and reassuring in Emma's existence, until and unless we begin to fret about the presence of the word "seemed" in this otherwise unruffled opening sentence. It insinuates a worrisome thought that beneath the surface "blessings" that grace Emma's existence important things are being concealed. Once this suspicion is aroused, it spreads throughout the novel like a contagion. Some of the symptoms are mild and indeed offer much-appreciated entertainment in the cloistered world of Highbury: the passion for puzzles and word games, idle conjectures about the hidden motives behind an unscheduled and apparently frivolous trip to London or the sudden appearance of a pianoforte in the parlor of a genteel family of limited means. Less innocent in this novel that traffics in minor but life-affecting mysteries is the prolonged social masquerades enacted by Frank Churchill and Jane Fairfax, who are secretly engaged but affect a mutual indifference. The most carefully guarded secret is the true inclination of Emma's own heart, a secret so well kept that its very existence is long unsuspected even by herself.

Let us not ignore, then, this verbal snag in the otherwise seamless garment outfitting Emma as she makes her entrance as the most richly endowed and self- confident heroine of the nineteenth century. It suggests that character itself may be a mystery hiding in plain sight, a suggestion that encourages us to divest Emma of her surface manner (with its real social, but questionable spiritual grace) in the hopes of uncovering, as she herself will do in the emotional climax of the novel, the actual disposition of her character and the real inclinations of her heart. Divest but not expose her. Getting to know such a character so well provisioned with beauty, brains, and wealth is not so much a question of stripping her down to her naked self – an existential ordeal Austen's heroines are largely spared – as coming to recognize and appreciate what is undeclared in her nature and unsettled in her fortune, not in her material fortune, of course, which is substantial, but in her prospects for happiness. Happiness, which is said to achieve perfection in her union with Mr Knightley, is literally the last word on human feeling in the novel. It is something *achieved* rather than bestowed by the accidents of birth. As such it represents quite a different emotional state than the self-contentment Emma enjoys throughout the novel until it collapses into moral chagrin at her own arrogant blindness in dealing with others and, as it turns out, with herself.

Such fine, but fateful discriminations between the rightfully happy and the foolishly, even wrongly self-contented character are not of urgent moral concern to Originals, who are not seekers of Happiness, but pursuers of Life. They only assume such importance for Individuals, for whom Happiness signifies the rightness of the life they have made for themselves. Even while we savor them, we know that most happy endings are lovely exercises in wish-fulfillment that allow us to escape from the messy and mixed reality of everyday existence. Still, happy endings are more than escapist fantasies; they fulfill a more sophisticated yearning to give one's life a proper, indeed its ideal, form. This yearning is embedded in the root sense of *individual*, a word that points us to the distinctive element or force in character that is indivisible, that resists absorption into some larger, encompassing social or cultural group. In Emma this desire initially takes the regressive form of resisting change and wanting to remain who and where she is – Emma Woodhouse, settled in her home in Hartfield (whose very name suggests her inclination to keep her affections close to home). Even a woman so richly advantaged as Emma is troubled by the fundamental problem of finding a social form that complements rather than compromises her deepest sense of who she is.

More than happiness, then, is achieved at the conclusion of *Emma*, just as more is celebrated than a series of marriages. What is fulfilled at the novel's close is a certain promise that Emma makes, we might say, to herself: to be true to herself. It is the promise Polonius advises Laertes to make to himself, and whether we consider it good or dismiss it as sententious advice does not make it any easier to decide what is involved in following it. For one thing, first you have to determine what the "truth" about yourself actually is. This is where the moral realism of novels proves invaluable, if not immediately reassuring. Novels, which aim to get at the truth of their characters, dramatize just how difficult it is to know oneself by presenting us with Individuals whose "truth" is often falsified by social masks or obscured by self-illusion, individuals, that is, who are as morally impenetrable to themselves as they are to others. For Henry James, the primary and exhilarating challenge of the novelist's art was to confront this opacity of individuals. In recounting his imaginative struggle to render the life and appeal of his "vivid individual," as he expressly calls his heroine, Isabel Archer, James reported that all his artistic and moral fretting over what form her story would take ultimately came down to one overriding question: "Well, what will she *do*?" (PL, p.51).

What indeed. There is, it seems, no telling, a real worry in a form that is all about finding ways of telling us the "true state" of things. James's novel justifies that worry and never manages to dispel it. If anything, James leaves his readers even more perplexed by the question of what Isabel will do at the end of the novel than at its beginning. I will return to the specific *content* of this worry later, for much rides on James's stubborn (some will find it his perverse) insistence that the question of what Isabel will do remain at the novel's close as unsettled as it ever was. There is much that is galling, even unnerving in not being *told* what will happen to her, but there is also something thrilling, as James insinuates, in being kept in such indefinite suspense. Novels that subordinate plot to the emotional adventures of Individuals traffic in a different, quieter but less easily resolved moral suspense. It is a suspense exemplified in "the anxiety, the curiosity" that Knightley, the man, besides her father, who has known and loved Emma the longest, feels in thinking about what will become of her.[2]

That this curiosity is attributed to a "knightley" character suggests that it is not of the vulgar sort, but the mark of a certain human refinement. Knightley, whose name carries the whiff of anachronism but not its odor of decay, is never more courteous than in his feeling *obliged* to admit the limits of his knowledge of Emma. This sense of obligation marks a new and unsettling attitude toward novelistic character. It entails the discomfiting recognition that no matter how much we are shown or told about characters, we can never be sure of what will become of them. Heroes and heroines no longer are served up to us "ready-made", to use Bakhtin's phrase for the hero of "the pre-dominant, mass type" who figure in most conventional novels. In these works, Bakhtin notes, "the hero sometimes attains, sometimes only approaches his goal: the bride, the victory, wealth, and so on. Events change his destiny, change his position in life and society, but he himself remains unchanged and adequate to himself."[3]

Bakhtin is primarily interested in what happens to the image of the hero when it is infused by historical time, that is, when the hero (or heroine) changes and becomes, as Emma does in the novel's psychological climax, *inadequate* to her deepest and most cherished sense of herself. He designates the type of novel committed to representing the hero or heroine in "the process of becoming" as "the novel of human *emergence*" (his italics), whose exemplary form is the *bildungsroman*, or novel of cultural formation. The *bildungsroman* is a form expressly developed to describe how the individual might succeed, although just as often fail, in achieving his or her goals, the highest and most elusive of which is what I have called one's true form. This dynamic idea of character, which echoes George Eliot's narrative assertion that "character is a process and an unfolding," is not, of course, limited to the *bildungsroman*, but extends to novels whose declared subject may be life in provincial societies (*Middlemarch)*, or the British class system (any classic realist novel, but especially those of Austen, Thackeray, Eliot, Gaskell, and Dickens), its ecclesiastical institutions (Trollope's Barchester chronicles) and political dynasties (his Palliser novels with its central, persisting figure, Phineas Finn), or the historical dislocations of modernity (any of Hardy's works beginning with *The Return of the Native*).

But whereas Bakhtin insists that "everything" in the drama of human emergence "depends upon the degree of assimilation of real historical time," I want to insist just as strongly on the way everything depends on the force *within* character, or rather – to invoke once again the Emersonian formulation – on character *as* the inner Force to resist as well as assimilate "real historical time." Not that this power to resist historical time ensures one's final victory over it. Novels, unlike romances or even epics, in which the gods have a stake in whether their heroes and heroines prosper or perish, know that reality, whether projected as Fate or Nature or History or Society, is as impersonal as it is remorseless in executing its decrees. Still, the novel is not an unmitigated record of acquiescence and defeat. It acknowledges but is not reconciled to Reality's implacable authority; it pleads the cause of those Quixotic characters who defy the established order of life. Sometimes this defiance extends to the very idea that characters are necessarily living within a novel and should abide by its internal laws. Forster makes this point comically, but with a certain irresistible point. Characters "arrive when evoked," he writes,

> but full of the spirit of mutiny. For they have these numerous parallels with people like ourselves, they try to live their own lives and are consequently often engaged in treasons against the main scheme of the book. They "run away," they "get out of hand." They are creations inside a creation and often inharmonious towards it; if they are given complete freedom they kick the book to pieces, and if they are kept too sternly in check, they revenge themselves by dying, and destroy it by intestinal decay.[5]

Thus the novelist's exasperation with some of his liveliest characters – they want to go their own way in defiance of the very "scheme" or formal power that gave them whatever life and role they may be said to possesses. They insist on their own meaning, even if, as it often is, it is inharmonious with the greater designs of the novel, and even if, as often happens, they leave the novel in shambles. At their most daemonic, as in the inflamed characters of Heathcliff, Rochester, Ahab, they are constitutionally mutinous, determined not only to run away from the novel, but *with* the novel, taking it into realms of thought and feeling where it has little chance of surviving – as a novel. They are in open revolt against the novel's subservience to the rude impositions of "reality." They rebel against social customs and moral traditions that have become so reified that they seem, even if they are not, the way things necessarily are and always will be. They rebel against any experience that does not belong in the eye of the beholder but in the controlling hands of an impersonal, abstract, and irresistible Power. Ahab sees Moby Dick as the most majestic and maddening and malevolent incarnation of that Power, but as George Eliot knew, it can express itself in more subtle, but equally malevolent and lethal ways in everyday concessions to the "false conformities" demanded by the conventions of social life. Wilde hoped to embolden us against it by deriding it as "that monstrous and ignorant thing that is called Public Opinion."[6]

This sense of character as "a process and an unfolding" that either fortifies or disintegrates its inner Force is what makes novelistic individuals appear morally opaque to others and to themselves. This opacity of character represents a moral as well as literary revolution in our conception of novelistic persons, as revolution that Iris Murdoch champions as the great achievement of nineteenth-century prose fiction.[7] But let us be clear, as Murdoch herself is, about the nature of this achievement. Murdoch's argument is based on the premise that "Literature must always represent a battle between real people and images."[8] We have seen how Originals like Don Quixote lust after images in their drive to remake reality into grander, often mythopoeic forms. The "real impenetrable human person" who morally excites Murdoch's imagination is different from those "great originators" (George Eliot calls them "the Shining Ones") who remain resplendent however far or near we are to them in time, in tradition, in temperament. Originals shine because they are lit from within, even if, as with Heathcliff and Ahab, that light resembles hellfire rather than the generative light of Genesis.

An individual like Emma, who embodies Murdoch's literary-moral ideal of the "real impenetrable human person" so fully imagined by the nineteenth-century novel, comes in and out of focus. Only in the final pages of the novel, through the intellectual and literary grace of an emergent novelistic device of free indirect discourse, does she become morally illuminated, finally and fully transparent to herself: "How to understand it all! How to understand the deceptions she had been thus praticising on herself and living under – the blunders, the blindness of her own head and heart!" (E, p.358). Within the next page and a half she does come to understand it all – well, as much as she needs to – and the sight leaves her, with the exception of her now acknowledged feeling for Knightley, disgusted. So we shouldn't take that flurry of exclamation marks as a sign of pleasant surprise, much less exultation at discovering the truth at last. They indicate a more dispiriting moment of self-astonishment, one befitting her mind's free fall into the depths of self-ignorance. Murdoch sees this outcome as morally salutary, since such moments confront us with "the hard idea of truth."[9] What is "the truth?" The truth, as Murdoch sees and calls it, that "we are benighted creatures sunk in a reality that we are constantly, and overwhelmingly tempted to deform by fantasy."[10]

Despite her quarrels with the Liberal conception of human character as fundamentally free and in possession of all that it needs to know to make informed and rational choices, Murdoch reminds us that the idea of the human person as "substantial, impenetrable, individual, indefinable, and valuable is after all the fundamental tenet of Liberalism."[11] In fact, individuality is not just the fundamental tenet of Liberalism. It is also its key word for expressing its moral conception of the human person as substantial, impenetrable, indefinable, and valuable. John Stuart Mill's quintessential Liberal tract, *On Liberty*, for example, confidently predicts that "if it were felt that the free development of individuality is one of the essentials of well-being ... there would be no danger that liberty should be undervalued, and the adjustment of the boundaries between it and social control should present no extraordinary difficulty."[12] A devoted reader of novels, especially one drawn to the *bildungsroman*, would question whether human development ever was or ever could be as free of difficulty as Mill envisions. To speak only of British characters who aspire to be the heroes and heroines of their own life: Becky Sharp, Jane Eyre, David Copperfield, Pip, Dorothea Brooke and Tertius Lydgate, Isabel Archer, Jude the Obscure – the lives of any of these self-seeking (and in Becky's case socially canny and rapacious) Individuals present concrete, often discouraging evidence of the extraordinary difficulty in negotiating the heavily patrolled boundaries between the developing character and social control.

These reservations reflect the rich accretions and complications of meaning attached to the idea of Individuals as it acquired its modern, common, and inherently *novelistic* meaning: singular and distinctive characters who assert themselves, with more or less confidence and success, within and often against the larger social consensus. Raymond Williams, who devotes one of his longest entries in *Keywords* to the changing senses of the word and its two most important modern offshoots – individualism and individuality – notes that "the development of the modern meaning from the original meaning is a record in language of an extraordinary social and political history."[13] With his characteristic breadth of reference and concise but never shallow summaries, Williams traces that history from its first memorable usage in Boethius and medieval theology, where it designates an essential indivisibility, through the eighteenth-century, where its "decisive development" into a "singular noun" occurs. The change does not originate, as we might expect, in religious or political thought, but in the formal classifications developed by logic and evolutionary biology that divide up genera into species, species into individuals.[14] Williams concludes by referring to Georg Simmel's important distinction between "the individualism of uniqueness – Einzigheit – as against that of singleness – Einzelheit." As Williams observes, the individualism of singleness is a quantitative concept; it posits the individual as an abstract integer, a concept that proved theoretically useful in the calculations of utilitarian ethics and statistics-based social sciences. The individualism of Uniqueness, on the other hand, is a qualitative conception; it designates what cannot be divided or duplicated and which resists assimilation into larger social or political units.

Let us turn to Simmel directly to make this distinction even more sociologically concrete and morally consequential:

> After the individual had been liberated in principle from the rusty chains of guild, hereditary status, and church, the quest for independence continued to the point where individuals who had been rendered independent in this way wanted also to distinguish themselves *from one another*. What mattered now was no longer that one was a free individual as such, but that one was a particular and irreplaceable individual.[15]

A constellation of values and their attendant social blessings began to form and orbit around the notion of individuality as a human ideal – freedom and self-dependence (allied but not necessarily the same thing), uniqueness, happiness in being who you are and were meant to be.

These ideals coalesce and are foregrounded in the definition of individuality that Simmel offers us: "a state of inner and external liberation of the individual from the communal forms of the Middle Ages, forms which had constricted the pattern of his life, his activities, and his fundamental impulses through homogenizing groups."[16] Hidden within these abstract formulations are the premises of a novel: the story, as we might envision it, of how an individual liberates herself from the family pressuring her from without and from the inhibitions constraining her from within. Because this story takes the form of a novel and not, for example, a romantic fable, we know how much fantasy colors our belief – or let us say our hope – that Individuals can become so morally independent that they only need answer to themselves. But we also know (at least we not unreasonably expect) that the novel, as a sponsor as well as recorder of the human desire and drive for freedom, is not disposed to dismiss this fantasy until it has been tested against the "real conditions" of everyday life.

Persuasions

Austen has a word for such forces that in their combined might can prove destructive of the moral and emotional integrity of individuals – Persuasion. She would devote her last novel to analyzing its moral effects. Her heroine, Anne Elliot, is Emma's successor but also her counterpart: Emma prides herself for her skill and tact in persuading, Anne is chagrined at being – or of having been – so persuadable. That they are both heroines alerts us to an important point: in the gender economy of the novel, the persuader occupies the masculine position of effective authority, while the persuaded is confined to an ever diminishing space where options are exhausted by small, often incremental and potentially fatal acts of compliance. Needless to say, characters of either sex can take up position in either of these moral territories. *Middlemarch's* fatal beauty, Rosamund Vincy, with her soft voice but tense neck, is the persuader in making and managing her marriage to Lydgate, who in turn proves to be the resistless object of her, and increasingly, of the world's persuasions.

The novel's heroes and heroines, those true Individuals in Mill's sense of that imposing word, must be alert and resistant to all forms of persuasion, even the most kindly meant. This moral conviction inspires the homely symbol that Austen, with her customary "playful solemnity," hazards in *Persuasion*. Captain Wentworth, Anne's past but resurgent love, is the first character to speak to the subject announced in the novel's title, arguing, as well he might, against persuadable character and for "the character of decision and firmness." "You are never sure of a good impression being durable. Everybody must sway it; let those who would be happy be firm."[17] A sensible maxim – let those who would be happy be firm. So sensible, indeed, that it might serve as the text for a parlor sampler, seen by anyone, but observed by few.

I would include Austen herself among those either tired or skeptical of aphorism. In *Persuasion* Austen seems to me increasingly dissatisfied with the perfunctoriness of maxims, however morally sound and whatever her own role in composing them. This would explain why she allows her moral imagination to venture into the Romantic woodlands where natural symbols grow, literally it would seem, on trees. At least this appears to be the case when Wentworth, speaking not to Anne but certainly about her, picks up a nut and proceeds to exemplify his point:

> a beautiful glossy nut, which, blessed with original strength, has outlived all the storms of autumn. Not a puncture, not a weak spot any where. This nut ... while so many of its brethren have fallen and been trodden under foot, is still in possession of all the happiness that a hazel-nut can be supposed capable of. (P, p.53)

Like Crusoe's seeds, Austen's homegrown nut contains the germ of parable. Indeed, in the very wistfulness of Wentworth's homily, we can detect how novelistic Individuals inherited but also transformed the forceful character of the Originals from whom they descend. In the novelistic Individual force of character is identified with the intrinsic strength to withstand external pressure. This strength is most often put to the test, especially but not exclusively in the case of women, in deciding who and even whether to marry. It is easy to see why the novel would see this decision as a test of character and not just a matter of sexual choice. Marriage is the ultimate personal test of whether the erotic and emotional happiness of persons coincides or interferes with the specific (often economic) interests of families. Emma's initial reluctance to consider marriage for herself reflects her moral awareness of what is at stake in marriage. She obviously prefers not to risk herself unless the rewards – perfect happiness as it turns out, lucky girl – are worth it. *Clarissa* remains the most profound as well as most harrowing account of how family, social, and economic interests can conspire and act like a juggernaut to grind individual wills into submission.

However, the more conventional (but not uninteresting or morally simple) test of character is who, not whether, to marry. The novel is as tireless as it is inventive in imagining what can happen when individuals, especially those who, like Dorothea Brooke or Isabel Archer, pride themselves in knowing what they are doing, marry on their own terms. Marriage may be the bourne of many a narrative, as Eliot somewhat pedantically reminds us at the conclusion of *Middlemarch*, but, as her own novels attest, it is also the route to unhappiness and, in extreme but not uncommon cases, to moral perdition. The emotional and social landscapes of the nineteenth-century novel are littered with the wreckage of marriages in which one or sometimes both partners entered into matrimony with eyes wide shut: Rawdon Crawley and Becky Sharp; David Copperfield and Dora, Dorothea and Casaubon, the Mayor of Casterbridge and the wife he sells into bondage, the sexual and self-mortifying union of Sue Bridehead and Phillotson – or the sheer catastrophe that marriage is for Gwendolen Harleth and Emma Bovary, driving one to virtual passive murder, the other to vengeful suicide.

But surely no heroine surpasses Isabel Archer in her splendid and fatal reliance on her own strong instinct in making her sexual choice. The first opportunity – she would call it the first temptation – presented to her as a heroine is to make a brilliant marriage with a "territorial, a political, a social magnate" with the imposing title of Lord Warburton. We are informed that Isabel, who is and knows herself to be "a character," makes her decision in response to "a certain instinct, not imperious, but persuasive, [that] told her to resist – murmured to her that *virtually* she had a system and an orbit of her own. (PL, p.156, my emphasis). Here instinct is given a voice and it speaks, as instinct generally does to strong-willed individuals, of resistance to the persuasions of public and all-too-common opinion. That the voice of instinct is described as murmuring rather than shouting is a sign of how quietly insinuating it can be. A louder instinct might alarm reason, but one that murmurs increases our inclination to "trust" it as the measured voice of sanity. So we should not be surprised that Isabel does trust this inner voice, even though it speaks, like an oracle, equivocally. It at once alerts her to the peril of being drawn into Lord Warburton's orbit and seduces her into believing that she has a system and can maintain an orbit of her own. Isabel, whose idea of her own individuality is allied to the moral idea of a "complete consciousness" of who she is and wants and requires, will discover the dreadful irony lurking in that "virtually" when her own system is absorbed into the orbit of a demon-husband who refuses to be persuaded by any consideration but his own.

This ironic outcome of Isabel's marriage plot suggests a different moral than Wentworth's "let those who would be happy be firm." It is "in character" for Individuals to proclaim and defend their own intactness, but it does not necessarily follow that the character impervious to all persuasions is necessarily a good one. It is important to heed this sobering qualification, but not to be limited or cowed by it. For despite such reservations, the novel tends to cheer on the Individual in his or her battle against the persuasions, most of them subtle and even friendly, but some of them brutal (especially in the novels of Charlotte Brontë and Dickens). In fact, viewed in this light – and it is not, I think, an hysterical or lurid light – Wentworth's image of a nut trodden under foot is not all that distant from Orwell's image of the human face crushed by jackboots in *1984*. What is destroyed in both instances is the idea, politically as well as spiritually empowering, of the inviolable, intact core at the heart of living, thriving things, be they nuts or what nuts are taken to exemplify – living people subject to external persuasion and often battered by the adversities of Life.

For Wentworth, whose name suggests that values can lapse as well as progress and grow over time, to be an Individual is to have the inner strength to resist all manner of persuasion, even those kindly meant, and to withstand the unpredictable but inevitable changes in our emotional and social environment. To retain this strength and survive the contingencies that alter and disrupt any life is the deepest and surest happiness individuals can know. John Stuart Mill pleads the same case for individuality "as One of the Elements of Well-Being," although in less poetic terms than Austen and with a more utilitarian notion of how to reckon happiness:

> It is desirable, in short, that in things which do not primarily concern others, individuality should assert itself. Where, not the person's own character, but the traditions or customs of other people are the rule of conduct, there is wanting one of the principal ingredients of human happiness, and quite the chief ingredient of individual and social progress.[18]

If we doubt that anyone can or even should secure the best blessings of existence on rampantly self-interested grounds, here is the very doctrine to alleviate our concerns. Mill argues against a prevalent feeling of his time and still current in ours, that the assertive individual and the collective good are in tension and at times antagonistic to each other, even "in things that do not primarily concern others." He not only insists that they do not interfere with each other; he warns that to inhibit or discourage individual development is to retard social progress. "While admitting that the energy of the strong character may be turned to bad uses" – think of that chilling villain Gilbert Osmond or the more complicated ambition driving the Mayor of Casterbridge – Mill maintains that

> [t]he same strong susceptibilities which make the personal impulses vivid and powerful, are also the source from whence are generated the most passionate love of virtue, and the sternest self-control. It is through the cultivation of these, that society both does its duty and protects its interests: not by rejecting the stuff of which heroes are made, because it knows not how to make them.[19]

Women of Character

The novel, needless to say, does know how to make them. What it makes *of* them is a much more complicated and intriguing story than Mill lets on. This story has no set moral, but it does have a set purpose – to create vital, if fictive human beings, people like ourselves, as Forster claims, who have all the recognizable qualities of people except a material body. Like us, they are sexed. This is an elementary fact about novelistic character whose meaning and importance have changed over time, remain controversial, cannot be underestimated, but should not be exaggerated. No one pretends that it doesn't matter, either in life or in art, whether you live your life as a man or a woman or some combination of the two. Yet to what degree sex determines who you are is another and much more stubborn (impossibly so!) question altogether.

Of all the authorities that have weighed in on the problem, only the novel tailors its answer to particular, if imagined cases. Novels show us how characters develop or deteriorate, flourish or wither, under certain very specific personal, social, and historical circumstances. Its specialized study of human development in concrete social and historical environments has had a disproportionate impact on how the character of women was and is represented. In exploring the vast tracts of everyday life "in its true state," the novel, in its most generous moods, offered women a great opportunity to show what stuff they are made of. Often what they have to show us is hardly what we might expect. They frequently are the novel's most surprising characters, defying conventions, acting against type, refusing, as Marcela does, the life of a paragon in order to pursue, protect, and preserve their own individuality.

So much the better for them. It is self-insistent force, whatever form it takes, that makes a character *into* a self-dependent individual. We now recognize and condemn the ideological disposition of patriarchal societies to make women *as a class* a general exception to that rule. Women, according to the rule and regime of patriarchy, ideally should confine their moral energy to the private sphere and act on everyone's behalf but their own. But time and the aberrant example of ungovernable women exposed the rule as unjust and oppressive, and in certain sublime instances, unenforceable. To speak only of their literary presence on the world-stage, women had shown what they were capable of in drama, where the strength and caliber of their character were put to the test and on public display. From Greek tragedy through the modern theater that extends from Shakespeare to Ibsen's problem dramas, the stage is home to vivid and powerful, willful, and unconventional, sex-confounding heroines – Clytemnestra, Antigone, Medea, Juliet and Rosalind, Phaedra, Millamant, Hedda Gabler, and Nora Helmer – heroines whose actions cannot always be said to serve society's interests nor even, in the most desperate circumstances, their own.

These heroines expressed but also exhausted their force upon the stage. *Don Quixote*, with its bands of roving women, some of them low but many of them born into the middle and higher ranks of Spanish society, promised to open up a new world for the heroines of epic and romance, who moved very little or seldom far from the places where Fate had first deposited them. They might be transported as marriage chattel or prizes of war, go on pilgrimages or retreat into nunneries, but they were hardly encouraged, like the pastoral lovers and runaway brides of the first book of *Don Quixote*, to take to the road in pursuit of fugitive loves or, like Marcela, to found a pastoral colony of one where she would never again be importuned to marry.

Yet the Quixotic freedom to roam beyond the limits of social and sexual convention was no sooner glimpsed than it was curtailed; only those of lowly status and questionable morals, like Moll

Flanders or Roxana or that sly upstart, Becky Sharp, seemed to move, if not always freely, farther afield than their more stay-at-home and better behaved sisters. The novel found it difficult to unburden itself of the sexual traditions erected and defended over millennia. Yet to its everlasting credit, it took up this burden as one of its central moral and social preoccupations. The novel acknowledged, as no other literary form did or could, that a general interdiction was in force that kept women at home or dictated the terms and the distance and purpose of their travel. The opening, resentful line of *Jane Eyre* speaks of this general interdiction on woman's freedom of movement in painfully personal and local terms: "There was no possibility of taking a walk that day." Character wants room, Emerson advised, but female characters born in traditional societies – that is to say most societies until the recent past – were discouraged from straying too far from their appointed place, unescorted, as it were, by the social retinue and trappings of femininity.

No one makes this feminist point with more bitterness, cunning, and malice than Madame Merle, the greatest villainess – but also among the greatest love-victims – of nineteenth-century fiction. Like her more appealing counterpart, Madame Vionnet, a less avid but equally desperate schemer after her daughter's future, Madame Merle is culturally and temperamentally a woman of the *ancien régime* translated into the modern world of mobile capital and shifting social alliances. Born before the French Revolution, Madame Merle – who is never known or called by her first name, as if her personal existence has been completely absorbed and camouflaged by her married, possibly bogus name – has spent her life trying to make a place in the new social and economic orders emerging in post-revolutionary, post-Napoleonic Europe. These new regimes underwrote and were in turn supported by the bourgeois, Liberal creed of self-development and its foundational, potent, and infectious myth of Great Expectations. As an historically, socially, and morally displaced person, Madame Merle, whose manner is at once so grand and enigmatic that Isabel at one point suspects that she might have once "aspired to wear a crown" (PL, p.252), has a sense of woman's lot that is destructive of this myth. As she tells Isabel: "... a woman, it seems to me, has no natural place anywhere: wherever she finds herself she has to remain on the surface and, more or less, to crawl. You protest, my dear? You're horrified? You declare you'll never crawl? It's very true that I don't see you crawling: you stand more upright than a good many poor creatures. Very good; on the whole, I don't think you'll crawl" (PL, p.248).

This exchange can make our own skin crawl, a sensation likely to recur with increasing frequency once Isabel settles in the "land of consideration" where her husband holds court, exhibiting "his tastes, his studies, his accomplishments, his collections" with the express purpose of "exciting the world's curiosity and then declining to satisfy it" (PL, p.444). And yet I myself wonder whether Madame Merle, even as she is unquestionably intent on luring Isabel into a sense of false security by venturing that "on the whole, I don't think you'll crawl," is not at the same time declaring her actual view of women's social fate. The two aims are not incompatible and indeed reinforce each other.

Isabel does not entertain this possibility – and the oversight will cost her. She is either too naïve or too preoccupied with her own quest for Life to consider Madame Merle a creditable interpreter of women's experience. She can hardly perceive, much less acknowledge the leagues that separate the Life she yearns for and the Existence that probably awaits her, as it awaits so many peripatetic women who wander over the surface of the earth seeking their fortunes with varying and highly volatile combinations of hope, courage, imagination, and ambition. Much depends, then, on how Madame Merle's "very good" sounds to our ears. It literally sounds as her sharp and definitive concession to Isabel as a woman of happier character and fortune than her own. To my ears, however, the words "very good" are the two blunt taps of Madame Merle's sinister irony testing the sturdiness of the trap she has so delicately and painstakingly prepared for Isabel to enter. Once ensnared in Madame Merle's deceitful plot, Isabel will spend the last agonizing section of the novel, that is, most of the days of her marriage, trying to stay upright against the considerable pressure of her husband to force her, morally speaking, to her knees.

Does she succeed? James notoriously leaves the question of Isabel's future suspended, literally, on a threshold where she receives – and then flees – the white lightning kiss that Caspar Goodwood had hoped would, as in a fairy tale, free her from the malignant enchanter who is her husband and deliver her over to himself. Those who subscribe to the American and Liberal doctrines of Individualism will fret about what James intends in the ostensible rout of Goodwood's fantasy. The meaning remains heartbreakingly ambiguous, although the outcome of Isabel's struggle to extricate herself from Caspar's embrace, is quite clear: "she was free." It is a freedom that is enjoyed, however, in darkness. Does this atmospheric detail mean that Isabel has reclaimed her individuality or lost it when she turns her back on Caspar Goodwood and puts her hand on the latch leading her away from the man who has followed and tormented her? Is she permanently abandoning her "very good" chance to join her life to a man who stands, as much as any man in this novel does, for uprightness – with all the stiffness, phallic as well as emotional and moral, that uprightness in this novel implies? So many of Isabel's movements are baffling, even to herself, that we can hardly tell whether her turning her back on Goodwood is an act of sexual flight or a spirited defense of her right to go to hell in her own way. The last words of the novel are "the key to patience" and while they immediately refer to Henrietta Stackpole's moral gift to the rebuffed Goodwood, the key itself could easily be the instrument Isabel will use, we fear, to lock herself in rather than let herself out.

Of course Madame Merle is damned and sees things from the vantage point of her own private historical hell. Not all heroines are forced to crawl over whatever social surfaces extend out before them. Still, it is virtually a convention of the realist novel that heroines must maintain a modest and morally decorous gait: they may stroll or amble, but never run, and certainly not gallop toward their own future. One of the great moral challenges facing the novelistic heroine is to move, often against vociferous objection, under her own power and in her own way. The good, but not necessarily nice, heroine moves at a pace that permits us to take stock of where she has been and where she might be going. That gadabout and globetrotter of *The Portrait of a Lady*, Henrietta Stackpole, who is described as having been "obliged to sacrifice her hopes with regard to the inner life" (PL, p.332), could never sit still long enough to be the subject of a portrait. No one can or should deny the courageous record of traveling heroines who disregarded convention to venture forth as confidently and as freely as the most well-equipped hero. But for those who value, as I do, spiritual as well as physical movement, not enough attention and praise have been bestowed on the heroines whose movements, like their lives, being restricted, found ways to circumvent or transcend the social and narrative codes designed to keep them in their place. Roland Barthes, wandering through the mazes of a lover's discourse, inevitably confronts these codes dictating sexual positions, roles, and opportunities and reduces them to their operative narrative axioms: "Woman is sedentary; Man hunts, journeys. Woman is faithful (she waits); Man is fickle (he sails away, he cruises)."[20] Women, according to these conventions, are enjoined, sometimes forced, simply to stay where they are and wait.

But for women of character, those heroines I consider to be true Individuals, waiting is never passive. One of the things that makes a heroine a heroine is knowing how to wait. Waiting becomes for her a space to weave her own plots (Penelope at her web, staving off suitors) or, less concretely but just as decisively, to conjure more resplendent images of who and where she wants to be. Heroines who know how to wait, which effectively means that they know what to wait for, show us how much Life can be experienced by sitting still. Their sedentary reveries prepare for the grand introspective quests of the modern novel. Life subsiding to predictable and numbing routine, heroines take advantage of the inactivity imposed upon them to come alive, as Beckett puts it, in mind,[21] mentally wandering through landscapes that rise up before their dreaming eyes. Beneath their quiet, placid, or seemingly resigned exterior, something momentous is taking place or being thought. This is Henry James's exact claim in pointing, with considerable pride, to Isabel's "extraordinary meditative vigil" as the best scene in *The*

Portrait of a Lady. He is obviously pleased in having caught his heroine's "vivid" individuality in a sedentary pose that, he insists, "throws the action further forward than twenty 'incidents' might have done":

> She sits up, by her dying fire, far into the night, under the spell of recognitions on which she finds the last sharpness suddenly wait. It is a representation simply of her motionlessly SEEING, and an attempt withal to make the mere still lucidity of her act as "interesting" as the surprise of a caravan or the identification of a pirate. It represents, for that matter, one of the identifications dear to the novelist, and even indispensable to him; but it all goes on without her being approached by another person and without her leaving her chair. (PL, pp. 54–5, emphasis in original)

Earlier in his preface James had wondered what his heroine would do. Apparently she never interests or surprises him more than when she does nothing more than simply sit in her chair. In the "mere still lucidity" of Isabel's absorption in her own thoughts, the impetus of Character towards self-expressive, self-realizing action is at once forestalled and driven inward. It is thus as much the dramatist as the portraitist in James who exults in having caught his heroine at the moment of stillness when all manner of important things are happening out of our sight but within our vision. This drama, *as* drama, will only interest us if we care or are in the presence of "vivid individuals" who can communicate their liveliness without stirring a muscle. It is a drama that relies less on incidents than on what James calls identifications – those acts of recognition or *anagnorisis* on which, according to Aristotle in the *Poetics*, the drama ideally turns.

This dramatic turn into the mind of character is associated with the steady and irreversible feminization of novelistic experience. Heroines who were enjoined by social and literary convention to wait, who were confined or morally entrapped by the social and sexual codes that limited their chance to wander, indeed to err, on their own, reacted by finding adventure – and the disaster as well as rush of life that can follow from it – within their own minds.

Novelistic heroines of the nineteenth century not only hold their own with heroes, but often outshine them as Individuals whose unique characters are to be celebrated for their moral power or, as in the case of Madame Bovary or Eustacia Vye, who also feels she would be fulfilled if only she could get to Paris, lamented as so much wasted force.

By and large it is women who inherit the Quixotic legacy in all its pathos as well as all its promise of self-transformation and emotional exaltation. The nineteenth-century novel abounds in morally timid heroes – any of Dickens's boy-heroes (Pip and David Copperfield), Lydgate, and Angel Clare – but it is the heyday of what Ellen Moers, in her indispensable study, *Literary Women*, termed "heroinism."[22] Heroinisms, to be accurate, for as Moers amply and eloquently demonstrates, female heroism expressed itself in many forms and guises: traveling heroinism, loving heroinism, performing heroinism, and educating heroinism. And then there is "bad" heroinism, a less savory but shamelessly exultant assertion of female force. Bad heroines are skillful either in exploiting or demolishing the social idealizations of male as well as female character. Becky Sharp is so relentless in defending her own interests that we may credit her, not Thackeray, as the source of the subtitle, a novel without a hero, so overmastering is her power over the male protagonists who are foolish enough to woo, wed, or oppose her. There is evidently no hero available or conceivable in Thackeray's imagination who is up to the job of getting the best of this irrepressible, self-insistent adventuress. Not even Thackeray has the courage or the heart to do it, and decides to pack up his puppet show and concede that she has, in fact, kicked his book to pieces, leaving its moral, if not in shambles, in a state of disarray.

These heroines live and sometime die or are damned according to the one great principle of novelistic character – that heroines are Individuals before they are women. Sex-consciousness does not determine, but complicates their sense of themselves as Individuals. Heroines possess and act according to the "same strong susceptibilities which make the personal impulses vivid and powerful" that distinguish the heroes who aspire to win them, rival them, or subdue them. This force that makes for character, that preserves and defends individuality, that makes the personal impulses vivid and powerful, expresses itself as a passion.

Aristocrats and Commoners

The supreme form of this passion is the Quixotic desire to redeem one's own time, a passion for the reformation of reality by which the world will be returned to its "true state" as an enchanted place. George Eliot naturalizes this passion by identifying it with a soul-hunger that sets the "mind struggling toward an ideal life" (M, p.3). *Middlemarch*, her most Quixotic novel, is almost clinical in analyzing the symptoms and consequences of this soul-hunger in the moral life of its heroine, Dorothea Brooke. Her sister, Celia, recognizes Dorothea's Quixotic character without understanding how it fuels her vague, but potent yearning for sublimity: "You always see what nobody else sees. It is impossible to satisfy you; yet you never see what is quite plain. That's your way, Dodo"(M, p.34). Seeing what nobody else sees and wanting what no one can have are defining traits of the Quixotic character. So is the blind fervor that can make Dorothea, like Don Quixote, strike out against those least expecting and often least deserving of it. *Middlemarch* opens with a somewhat tart comedy of embarrassed courtship when a spiritually haughty Dorothea dismisses the patient and quite earnest approaches of Sir James, a situation Henry James would remember and replay, with less emphasis on the comedy of spiritual misalliance, in Isabel's refusal of Lord Warburton.

Dorothea's ardor, like Emma's cleverness, is, then, a mixed blessing and, again like Emma, for all her moral energy (however well or ill directed) nothing magnificent is to be expected of her. This, however, is precisely what interests Eliot about her heroine. She declares as much when she warns us in the novel's Prelude that her heroine will not, like that ecstatic Original and administrative genius, St Teresa, find for herself an "epic life wherein there was a constant unfolding of far-resonant action"(M, p.3). Eliot, who adopts the narrative persona of social historian, sees the causes of her heroine's apparently blundering "life of mistakes" as "the offspring of a certain spiritual grandeur ill-matched with the meanness of opportunities." I was once moved by this account of Dorothea's historical predicament, but now I am inclined to reject its determinism as dangerously close to a moral alibi. Over time I have been, perhaps wrongly, educated and persuaded by less resigned conceptions of what "life in its true state" might offer us in the way of adventure and sublimity. Think only of the parched landscapes of La Mancha, the meanness of opportunities and of the meals in which Don Quixote's soul-hunger found nourishment.

So I urge that we not concede too quickly the conclusion that Eliot reaches at the close of the novel in pronouncing that "the medium in which the ardent deeds" of Originals like St Teresa and Antigone is "for ever gone" (M, p.784). Although Eliot had initially recommended her novel to those interested in the "varying experiments of Time," she now seems to be declaring the experiment, at least the most humanly exciting phase of it, at an end. This is so absolute and so disheartening a verdict against the present and any future Time that only the most pessimistic chroniclers of the human experiment would endorse it. But it is a verdict that proves determinative for Eliot's art and indicates what her moral realism was willing to sacrifice – the transformative presence of Originals. Originals *make* the world – even if it is as arid as the landscapes of La Mancha or the stony, unpopulated island where Crusoe is washed ashore – into the medium of their self-transfiguration.

However much energy, excitement, and hope is lost by their omission from the human scene, Eliot clearly believes it is worth the sacrifice. It leaves her free to devote her attention to the vagaries of individual characters, only two of whom possess the stuff of heroes: Dorothea, another provincial heroine who is "remarkably clever," handsome, and rich, although, unlike Emma, driven by a religious rather than artistic yearning to improve the destinies of mankind; and Lydgate, the newcomer to Middlemarch who brings with him all the best modern ideas and medical advances. In any other novel, we would expect them to find their way to each other as lovers, but Eliot's moral scheme has other partners and destinies in mind for them. Dorothea's misdirected ardor leads her into a marriage that depresses, but finally cannot undo her. Lydgate's ardor, being more intellectual than spiritual, finds a worthy human object in medical reform, but is squandered and then extinguished in a marriage and social alliances that fatally compromise him. The difference in their fortunes may be ascribed to the difference between a woman who insists on seeing what no one else sees – like a husband in a desiccated pedant – and acts as no one else acts – like giving up a fortune to marry a man without rank, money, or any settled prospects; and a man who despite his uncommon gifts and sophisticated tastes can neither value nor desire anything that has not first been marked out by others as worth his while.

Both Dorothea and Lydgate will depart Middlemarch and eventually "disappear" into unrecorded history, but that does not mean that there is no larger historic significance to their stories. In Dorothea's "success" as a human being and Lydgate's failure in his, if not the world's, estimation, Eliot dramatizes not just the moral appeal but the social impact of the quixotic conception of nobility as spiritual distinction. This conception is at the moral core of Dorothea's character, as Eliot presents her. Indeed we may think of her character as exemplifying a unique sublimation of the most important social legacy of quixotism – the separation of the noble personality from established aristocratic structures and institutions. Although it presents itself to us as a provincial history of England between the passage of the first and second Reform Bill, *Middlemarch* can also be profitably read as an historical allegory of class consciousness (as a novelist like Eliot, rather than a dialectical materialist like Marx understands consciousness) that describes the submergence of aristocratic natures into the undifferentiated expanses of common, rather than epico-historic life. Submergence, not disappearance. For it is Eliot's conviction, and the ground of her most consistent social hopes, that "finely-touched spirits" like Dorothea contribute in invisible and unrecognized ways to the "growing good" of the world.

In Dorothea's "finely-touched spirit" we can track the migration and metamorphosis of the aristocratic into the Individual character. This development is accompanied, as we might expect, by a transfer, but also a transvaluation of aristocratic values. It is a development recounted with ferocious and subversive wit by Nietzsche in passages like this from his *Genealogy of Morals*, in which he defines the genesis and self-directed evolution of the aristocratic system of values:

> It acts and grows spontaneously, it merely seeks its antithesis in order to pronounce a more grateful and exultant "yes" to its own self; its negative conception, "low," "vulgar," "bad," is merely a pale late-born foil in comparison with its positive and fundamental conception (saturated as it is with life and passion), of "we aristocrats, we good ones, we beautiful ones, we happy ones."[23]

Nietzsche's aristocrat, rejoicing in his own nature, personifies and possesses all the attributes – nobility, goodness, beauty – required to translate the individual out of the realm of the common, the low, the vulgar, the bad, the ugly, the mean-spirited – all cognates, Nietzsche argues, for unhappiness[24] – into its own fine sphere of self-realizing action. D. H. Lawrence, who inherited and reacted to this Nietzschean idea of aristocratic character, offered a more prosaic, but equally fervent affirmation of the individual over what he calls "the undistinguished bourgeois or average being." By individualist, he insists, "is meant, not a selfish or greedy person, anxious to satisfy appetites, but a man of distinct being, who must act in his own particular way to fulfill his own individual nature. He is a man who, being beyond the average, chooses to rule his own life to his own completion, and as such is an aristocrat." And then, as if reporting the most shopworn truism rather than, as he is, issuing a startling judgment, Lawrence concludes: "The artist always has a predilection for him."[25]

But sometimes an artist does not indulge her predilection, at least not in all cases. Dorothea seems coddled when compared with the infirmity of will and self-disappointment Eliot exposes in Lydgate.

Of course Dorothea doesn't think of herself in aristocratic terms, while Lydgate, we soon learn, hardly thinks of himself in any other way. We are advised by Eliot's moralizing narrator that it is precisely this spiritual pride that will sink him into a common, though never vulgar state of "discontented subjection." Eliot anticipates how difficult her moral analysis of her hero might be for her readers to understand, much less accept. She makes several attempts to explain and enforce her own moral viewpoint, most memorably in presenting her distinguished hero as morally blemished by what she famously identified and diagnosed as "spots of commonness." "How could there be any commonness," she asks with her customary flash of irony,

> in a man so well-bred, so ambitious of social distinction, so generous and unusual in his views of social duty? As easily as there may be stupidity in a man of genius if you take him unawares on the wrong subject, or as many a man who has the best will to advance the social millennium might be ill-inspired in imagining its lighter pleasures.... Lydgate's spots of commonness lay in the complexion of his prejudices, which, in spite of noble intention and sympathy, were half of them such as are found in ordinary men of the world; that distinction of mind which belonged to his intellectual ardour, did not penetrate his feeling and judgment about furniture, or women, or the desirability of its being known (without his telling) that he was better born than the country surgeons. (M, pp. 141–2)

Here is evidence, if we are in the mood to accept it, that Individualist ardor, unlike the passion of Originals, tends to be self-limiting; it cools or is soon exhausted. Lydgate's intellectual ardor dissipates on the permeable border that separates the solitary self from the social realm of persuasions. He takes his values, as Nietzsche might say, from the herd of ordinary men; distinction for him is reduced to a fashion – in furniture or in women whose obvious beauty has little, if any, of the "finely-tuned" spirit attending it.

Lydgate's commonness is thus of no common sort; it is the paradoxical expression and moral consequence of his most cherished sense of himself as a man of distinction. His very desire that it be known, without his telling, that he is better born, more talented, and more sophisticated than the country surgeons among whom he lives and practices, will eventually debase him. Instead of realizing himself as an Individual, he condemns himself to the ranks of those ambitious men who "once meant to shape their own deeds and alter the world a little" but instead came to be "shapen after the average and fit to be packed by the gross" (M, p.135). This is a devastating comedown for Lydgate and Eliot shows a fine sarcasm in describing it, one that reveals her own aristocratic disdain for those who pretend to an inbred distinction that they sorely lack. She seems genuinely piqued at the moral stupidity of her splendid egotist-hero and so lumps him with those who have surrendered the two hard-won attributes of Individuality – singleness and uniqueness – and are now only fit to be packed by the gross.

It is a momentary flare-up, however, and Eliot's narrator moves on to more temperate reflections on how "you and I may have sent some of our breath towards infecting" the Lydgates of the world with commonness "when we uttered our conforming falsities or drew our silly conclusions"(M, p.135). A good deal of the plot of *Middlemarch* centers on the establishment of a fever hospital, but the story concerns the more endemic contagion of social life itself, with its conforming falsities, silly conclusions, and its predilections for inherited and traditional habits over individual experiments in self-fashioning.

In *Great Expectations* this contagion takes the form of a diseased dream in which all existing vectors of social direction and distinction are reversed and upended. The seeds of the nightmare are sown in Pip's first confused fantasies about his parents, which he derives from the "character and turn" of the inscriptions on their tombstones. A mere child, it seems, can intuit the uncanny relation between the modern idea of character and the Greek word for an engraved sign. We are not told if the lettering on the tombstones is Gothic, but it doesn't need to be; the character of the family legend is gloomy and dispiriting enough. It is a legend that poses the riddle of origins and "the identity of things" in terms of place: his father at the head, his mother, "Also Georgiana, wife of the Above," below, surrounded by a row of five nondescript "lozenges" that are the only surviving traces of the siblings "who gave up trying to get a living, exceedingly early in that universal struggle" (GE, p.3).

It is against and within this landscape of death that Pip first becomes aware of himself as a distinct "character," shivering and crying with fear, caught in the grip of the escaped convict, Magwitch, who threatens to slit his throat. The plot of *Great Expectations* may be said to begin, morally speaking, at the moment that Magwitch turns Pip upside down, emptying his pockets in search of money and food. All that follows in the novel may be said to result from Pip's efforts to reclaim his "upright" position after Magwitch has turned him, hence his vision of things, "head over heels." For not just Pip's body, but his moral universe is overturned by this sudden encounter with a hungry and menacing specter who looms up out of the darkness, an agent and victim of all that is wrong and guilty in the world.

As it transpires, nothing in Pip's subsequent education makes such an impression upon him as this traumatic lesson in the moral significance of the placement of things: above and below, up or down, high and low. It becomes his way of ascertaining who as well as where one is in the social order and, ultimately, in the moral scale of being. It fuels his dread of remaining mired in the culture of "lowness" to which Estella condemns him when she pronounces him common and coarse and "generally.... in a low-lived bad way" (GE, p.65). It connects him, in ways that he does not foresee but that will eventually appall him, to Magwitch's own dream of "raising" him to the rank of a high-living gentleman. It links both his own hopes of great expectations and Magwitch's ambitions for him to the preeminent fable of the child's fantasy life – the family romance.[26] This is the fantasy Freud uncovered in the depths of the child's unconscious, a fantasy in which a child imagines a more flattering, self-ennobling story about its own origins, in which the insufferably ordinary parents are replaced by those of noble, even royal lineage. This fantasy is at once doubled and inverted in what we might call the Magwitch fantasy of fatherhood, in which one imagines oneself giving birth to a son more noble than oneself.

Great Expectations is a novel of bitter, but necessary disillusionment that links the moral regeneration of character to the relinquishing of such fantasies of ennoblement. If Dickens secretly harbors the *predilection d'artiste* for the aristocrat, he does his best to curb it. This is a clue to the curious vitality and astounding variety of his characters, flat and round, major and minor, high and low. They do not assert themselves out of an aristocratic fullness of being and pride of life. Even complicated, if minor characters like Jaggars may have extraordinary power over the lives of others, but their own characters are drawn, as it were, defensively, almost as if Dickens were protecting them from his reader's own great and baseless expectations that characters can always be reduced to easily recognizable and scrutable types. Dickens's characters, however one-dimensional they may at times appear, remain fundamentally inscrutable. They shield themselves – or rather, let us say Dickens shields them – from scrutiny. They conceal the deepest – or most shallow? – reality of their character behind the social screen provided by a signature phrase ("I will never desert Mr Micawber" being, I suspect, the most famous) or an idiosyncratic gesture. But the very traits or behaviors that serve as trademarks safeguarding their individuality also imprison them, like Miss Havisham, in a timeless chamber from which there seems to be no exit. Joyce was not the first or last, but certainly he was among the most eloquent in noting how every character in Dickens appears to us "in the light of one strongly marked or even exaggerated moral or physical quality – sleepiness, whimsical self-assertiveness, monstrous obesity, disorderly recklessness, reptile-like servility, intense round-eyed stupidity, tearful and absurd melancholy." It was precisely this "one strange, wayward moral or physical deformity," Joyce observed, that transports his "fundamentally natural and probable" characters "from the world of tiresome reality and as far as the borderland of the fantastic."[27]

Joyce, instantly recalling the warmth of life in Dickens's most stunted characters, quickly amends himself and places Dickens's characters on the border of the Human Fantastic. That is, indeed, where we usually find them. But even Dickens realizes the dangers of leaving them there, in all their agitated and often helpless individuality. Unassisted by his own sympathetic imagination for the odd and eccentric, they could easily degenerate into a set of depersonalizing behaviors. This is precisely what happens to the already questionable character of Magwitch, whose criminal past resists all Pip's attempts to disguise it. As Pip comes to fear, "from head to foot there was Convict in the very grain of the man." "In all his ways of sitting and standing," Pip despairs,

> and eating and drinking – of brooding about, in a high-shouldered reluctant style – of taking his great horn-handled jack-knife and wiping it on his legs and cutting his food – of lifting light glasses and cups to his lips, as if they were clumsy pannikins – of chopping a wedge off his bread, and soaking up with it the last fragments of gravy round and round his plate, as if to make the most of an allowance, and then drying his finger-ends on it, and then swallowing it – in these ways and a thousand other small nameless instances arising every minute in the day, there was Prisoner, Felon, Bondsman, plain as plain could be. (GE, pp. 337–8)

A method actor might envy Pip's powers in observing those tell-tale behaviors that in a thousand small but obvious ways indelibly mark Magwitch's character as a felonious one. The problem is that these tell-tale signs tell much too simple a tale. Pip has caught Magwitch in his conditioned behaviors, but has not drawn him to the life. He is reading Magwitch through the language of low-lived types that makes his character socially visible but that cannot begin to capture what is personally distinctive about the story he carries within him. Standing or sitting, Magwitch seems at this moment as fit as he ever will be to be packed by the gross and shipped off to the land of the Average rather than Fantastic Man. In his shadow, we might catch a glimpse of the Totalitarian Man of the future, stripped of the last vestige of individual impulse or force, capable only of conditioned, Pavlovian responses.

The Incomparables

There are, famously, two endings to *Great Expectations*, one happy in the conventional way, one unresolved and darkly troubled in the best modern way. We can also read the ending as portending a tremendous divide in the moral evolution of Individuals, one leading down the road of Convention that, in its darkest turn, culminates in the totalitarian obliteration of individuality; the other taking us over the border of "life in its true state" into the realm of the Human Fantastic, where Nietzsche's *Ubermensch* waits to be born.

Still, the nineteenth century was the great epoch of Individuals and never lacked, even in its waning, artists determined to keep straight to the path blazed by Individuals. Among the most notable was Oscar Wilde. In his ebullient, almost giddy prophetic tract, *The Soul of Man Under Socialism*, Wilde envisions a Socialist utopia in which no one owns property but everyone can lay claim to himself. It is not the emancipation from material want, but much needed relief "from the sordid necessity of living for others" that Wilde promotes as the "chief advantage that would result from the establishment of Socialism" (Soul, p.137). This, as it turns out, is somewhat negatively expressed. Wilde is less interested in being freed from the necessity of living for others than in securing the positive freedom of living for oneself. This is the freedom that only Socialism can secure for the Individual, since, as Wilde understands and explains it,

> the recognition of private property has really harmed Individualism, and obscured it, by confusing a man with what he possesses. It has led Individualism entirely astray. It has made gain not growth its aim. So that man thought that the important thing was to have, and did not know that the important thing is to be. The true perfection of man lies, not in what man has, but in what man is. (Soul, p.132)

This argument lands us in a thicket of Wildean paradoxes: Socialism, a materialist, collectivist ideology and system of government, alone can secure and protect the right of the Individual to be left alone, absorbed in the only meaningful and purely spiritual work of self-perfection.

Wilde no sooner advances this paradoxical alliance of Socialism and Individualism than he proposes another. Although he will ultimately pronounce the new Individualism brought forth in Socialism as the new Hellenism, his vision of spiritual reflowering might as easily be called the new Christianity, so dependent is his vision of the "soul of man under socialism" on the Christian sacralization of the individual life as uniquely valuable and beloved in itself. "'Know thyself' was written over the portal of the antique world," Wilde proclaims in his most audacious prophecy. "Over the portal of the new world, 'Be thyself' shall be written." This, he declares, is "the message of Christ," the secret communicated in the third Beatitude – Blessed are the poor in spirit for theirs is the kingdom of heaven – whose meaning and intent he obligingly interprets for us: "When Jesus talks about the poor he simply means personalities, just as when he talks about the rich he simply means people who have not developed their personalities" (Soul, p.135)

There is, as Wilde well knew, nothing "simple" about what Jesus "meant" in this most baffling of the Beatitudes. His language may be relaxed and reassuring, but his interpretation is as heretical as Quixote's inverted beatitude, which also exalted those rich in being. For Wilde the "poor in spirit" are those rich in personality, using the word in the sense Dr Johnson defines it in his *Dictionary* – as "the individuality of anyone." In their perfected form these personalities represent and add to the wealth of the human tradition. Wilde opens *The Soul of Man Under Socialism* by invoking their names and example: "Now and then, in the course of the century, a great man of science, like Darwin; a great poet, like Keats; a fine critical spirit, like M. Renan; a supreme artist, like Flaubert, has been able to isolate himself, to keep himself out of reach of the clamorous claims of others, to stand 'under the shelter of the wall,' as Plato puts it, and so to realize the perfection of what was in him, to his own incomparable gain, and to the incomparable and lasting gain of the whole world"(Soul, p.127). The particular stress and meaning Wilde gives to the world "incomparable" is akin to the precision Melville brings to his definition of originals. Wilde, however, gives more emphasis and seems more dazzled by the singularity of those whose own gain is the world's gain. Mill had argued the same possibility, but with the condition that individuals acting in their own interest must not harm others. Wilde dismisses such concerns as morbid. Man, he argues in his peroration, "has sought to live intensely, fully, perfectly. When he can do so without exercising restraint on others, or suffering it ever, and his activities are all pleasurable to him, he will be saner, healthier, more civilised, more himself"(Soul, p.160).

Of course in *The Picture of Dorian Gray* Wilde had imagined a completely different outcome if those intent on living intensely were allowed to do so without restraint. But then *The Picture of Dorian Gray* is a novel that, as novels inevitably do, puts cherished theories to the test of experience. Experience teaches Dorian Gray a rather different lesson in soulcraft, as Dorian confesses just before his final murder and self-slaughter: "the soul is a terrible reality. It can be bought and sold and bartered away. It can be poisoned, or made perfect."[28] *The Soul of Man Under Socialism* appeared a year after the publication of *The Picture of Dorian Gray*. One wonders if Wilde was frightened by his own vision of spiritual servitude and hoped to argue himself, as well as us, into a less haunted consciousness of the soul, whether or not it abides under Socialism.

In the specter of Dorian's spiritual rot, the Individual becomes a horror to itself. It is the horror that Kurtz, that man of "no restraint," discovers in the darkness of his own voracious egoism, the very glimpse of which drives Marlow to seek refuge in a lie (as having the same, but less intense stink of mortality). This horror becomes the stuff of myth in Robert Louis Stevenson's tale of spiritual terror, *The Strange Case of Dr Jekyll and Mr Hyde*. The story opens with a chapter called "Story of the Door," a title that should alert us that this is to be a tale about moral and psychological thresholds and the danger of crossing them. It is not a story that can begin with any old door, but only on the threshold of *the* door that leads to the laboratory where Dr Jekyll conducts experiments on himself.

Before we cross into that dark interior, Stevenson reminds us of what lies on this side of door, of the certainties of character we must abandon once we enter there. With the easy mastery that would endear him to talents as different as Henry James and Borges, Stevenson opens with a character sketch in the best realist style:

> Mr. Utterson the lawyer was a man of a rugged countenance that was never lighted by a smile; cold, scanty and embarrassed in discourse; backward in sentiment; lean, long, dusty, dreary and yet somehow lovable. At friendly meetings, and when the wine was to his taste, something eminently human beaconed from his eye; something indeed which never found its way into his talk, but which spoke not only in these silent symbols of the after-dinner face, but more often and loudly in the acts of his life. He was austere with himself; drank gin when he was alone, to mortify a taste for vintages; and though he enjoyed the theater, had not crossed the doors of one for twenty years. But he had an approved tolerance for others; sometimes wondering, almost with envy, at the high pressure of spirits involved in their misdeeds; and in any extremity inclined to help rather than to reprove. "I incline to Cain's heresy," he used to say quaintly: "I let my brother go to the devil in his own way." In this character, it was frequently his fortune to be the last reputable acquaintance and the last good influence in the lives of downgoing men. And to such as these, so long as they came about his chambers, he never marked a shade of change in his demeanour.[29]

In retrospect, this description of character seems like a farewell to the full-blooded realist fiction that can bring the Individual so completely and engagingly to life: in his physical features, in his moral countenance, in his social behaviors, even, it is hinted, in his sexual reticence. Complete and centered: but this is a story, as Utterson's own name suggests, of extremities; it wants to visit the "uttermost" limits of the human, a limit that can be reached only by following the trail blazed by downgoing men like Dr Jekyll.

The downgoing man (a horror version of Lydgate) is literalized in Stevenson's faultless allegory, which figures Dr Jekyll's discovery of his inner and other half as a ghastly physical transformation that puts the human image in jeopardy. Everything in Hyde announces a terrible debasement of the "eminently human" – the reduction in stature (he is short and slight), the animal gait (he creeps like an ape), and the loss of a distinctive moral "countenance" (Hyde's face, even in Utterson's nightmares, lacks all individual features except for "the evil written broadly and plainly upon it"). And yet when Jekyll first sees (what no one else clearly does) the face of the "ugly idol" his soul cannot help but respond with "a leap of welcome": "This, too, was myself" (Jekyll, p.58).

Of course more is mirrored in this terrible, but exhilarating moment of self-greeting than Dr Jekyll's dark double and secret sharer. As Jekyll himself relates in his own presentation of his strange case, Hyde is both what he knows about himself and the limits of that knowledge:

> With every day, and from both sides of my intelligence, the moral and the intellectual, I thus drew steadily nearer to that truth by whose partial discovery I have been doomed to such a dreadful shipwreck: that man is not truly one, but truly two. I say two, because the state of my own knowledge does not pass beyond that point. Others will follow, others will outstrip me on the same lines; and I hazard the guess that man will be ultimately known for a mere polity of multifarious, incongruous and independent denizens. (Jekyll, pp. 55–6)

The catastrophe that Jekyll brings on himself is imaged as a dreadful shipwreck. The image reminds us that Crusoe, too, was a self-destroyer. And like Crusoe, Dr Jekyll works to salvage what he can from the wreckage. What he retrieves from his dreadfully misconceived investigations into his own character is nothing more solid than a guess, but it is an educated guess and will in fact prove to be a good one. For other novelists will follow Stevenson along these same lines of psychological investigation and discover that the Individual is divisible not just into two, but into many parts, that the inner character is less a "fortress of identity" than a polity, a commonwealth of multifarious, incongruous, and independent denizens. These denizens will become familiar to us under their common name – Selves.

Endnotes

1 Jane Austen, *Emma* (New York: Penguin, 1996), p. 7. Hereafter E.

2 Emma's father, like Anne Elliot's in *Persuasion*, takes his daughter's existence for granted, although his self-preoccupation is comic, whereas Mr Elliot's obliviousness relegates his daughter to a personal and social nullity. The narrator reports that Anne is regarded as a "nobody" within her own family, an existential demotion that the novel imaginatively labors to repair until its emotionally recessive heroine emerges as a somebody worthy of notice, commanding respect and inspiring love.

3 Mikhail Bakhtin, "The *Bildungsroman* and Its Significance in the History of Realism (Toward a Historical Typology of the Novel), *Speech Genres and Other Late Essays*, translated by Vern W. McGee (Austin: University of Texas Press, 1986), p. 20.

4 E. M. Forster, 1954, p. 97.

5 Oscar Wilde, *The Soul of Man Under Socialism and Selected Critical Prose*, ed. Linda Dowling (New York: Penguin, 2001), p. 147. Hereafter Soul.

6 Iris Murdoch, "Against Dryness," *Existentialists and Mystics* (New York: Penguin, 1997), pp. 291 passim.

7 Murdoch, 1997, p. 295.

8 Murdoch, 1997, p. 290.

9 Murdoch, 1997, p. 291.

10 Murdoch, 1997, pp. 294–5.

11 John Stuart Mill, *On Liberty and Other Essays* (Oxford: Oxford University Press, 2008), p. 63.

12 Raymond Williams, 1985, p. 133.

13 Williams, 1985, p. 135.

14 Georg Simmel, "Freedom and the Individual," *On Individuality and Social Forms* (Chicago: University of Chicago Press, 1972) p. 222.

15 Simmel, 1972, p. 217.

16 Jane Austen, *Persuasion* (New York: Penguin, 2003), p. 81. Herafter P.

17 Mill, 2008, p. 63.

18 Mill, 2008, p. 67.

19 Roland Barthes, *Lover's Discourse* (New York: Hill and Wang, 1979), p. 13.
20 Samuel Beckett, *Murphy* (New York: Grove, 1957), p. 2. Hereafter Murphy.
21 See Ellen Moers, *Literary Women* (New York: Doubleday, 1976). pp. 171–336 passim.
22 Friedrich Nietzsche, *The Birth of Tragedy and The Genealogy of Morals*, translated by Francis Golffing (New York: Doubleday Anchor, 1956), pp. 163, 172.
23 "For example, we should not fail to hear the almost benevolent nuances which for a Greek noble lay in all the words with which he set himself above the lower people – how a constant form of pity, consideration, and forbearance is mixed in there, sweetening the words, to the point where almost all words which refer to the common man finally remain as expressions for 'unhappy,' 'worthy of pity' (compare *deilos [cowardly], deilaios [lowly, mean], poneros [oppressed by toil, wretched], mochtheros [suffering, wretched]* – the last two basically designating the common man as a slave worker and beast of burden) – and how, on the other hand, for the Greek ear the words 'bad,' 'low,' 'unhappy' have never stopped echoing a single note, one tone colour, in which 'unhappy' predominates" (Nietzsche, 1956, p. 172).
24 Nietzsche, 1956, p. 439.
25 Peter Brooks discusses the centrality of this fantasy in the novel in *Reading for the Plot* (Cambridge: Harvard University Press, 1992), pp. 113–42.
26 James Joyce, "The Centenary of Charles Dickens," *James Joyce: Occasional, Critical and Political Writings*, ed. Kevin Barry (Oxford: Oxford University Press, 2000), pp. 185–6.
27 Oscar Wilde, *The Picture of Dorian Gray* (New York: Penguin, 2003), p. 205.
28 Robert Louis Stevenson, *The Strange Case of Dr Jekyll and Mr Hyde and Other Tales of Terror* (New York: Penguin, 2002), p. 5. Hereafter Jekyll.

II

Fractions

4

Selves/Identities

Somewhere between the time Dr Jekyll drank the potion that transformed him into a fiend and the moment Mr Leopold Bloom kindly set out a bowl of morning milk for his cat, human character changed. Virginia Woolf, in one of her more mischievous pronouncements declared that the change occurred "In or about December, 1910." The very arbitrariness of the date is what recommends it to Woolf, who amiably concedes that she hardly means to suggest that "one went out, as one might into a garden, and saw that a rose has flowered, or that a hen had laid an egg."[1] Changes *within* character, alas, do not announce themselves with such a definitive flourish, although one does want to keep one's eye on that egg, seeing what it will hatch.

Dr Jekyll's experiments on himself can be seen as a desperate attempt to force this change, to induce, as it were, a mutation in human character by artificial and accelerated means. Scientifically intrigued and personally distressed by "the thorough and primitive duality of man," Jekyll had hoped to personify, in order to separate out, those inner compulsions that threatened his psychic as well as his moral integrity. It was an integrity that seemed second nature to the great Originals and Individuals of the novel who preceded him. For this, as I have been arguing, is how the Originals and the Individuals of the novel impress us – a nimbus of integrity envelops them; they are not just singularly, but *invariably* who they are. Originals, especially of the Quixotic disposition, inevitably err, but they seldom stray very far from themselves. Their path is illuminated, as we have seen, from within; they follow their own nature, which manifests itself as a luminous Force that can be diminished or deluded in its aspirations, but never totally eclipsed. Hence George Eliot's name for them – the Shining Ones.

Individuals, on the other hand, are known less by their radiance than by their vividness. They are distinct beings who stand out, morally, from those average characters "fit," —in George Eliot's mordant phrase – "to be packed by the gross." Unlike Originals, who do not so much develop as discover themselves, Individual characters *unfold*. While they can betray their deepest sense of who they are, they remain, even in moral defeat or disgrace, wholly themselves. They may, like Lydgate, fail to "complete" their development, or they may wither and die in the bud, like Little Father Time, Hardy's despairing figure of age masquerading as juvenility. But they never inwardly entertain, as Bernard in *The Waves* routinely does, "shadows of people one might have been; unborn selves."[2] Individuals could never imagine being other than themselves and still remain Individuals.

The "strange case," as Stevenson designates it, of Dr Jekyll and Mr Hyde, was a harbinger of a breakdown in character from which the novel is yet to, and may never, recover. The fate of Jekyll may be lurid, but it is hardly a rare demonstration that the morally grand aim of the *bildungsroman* – to achieve a fully integrated individuality – no longer appears a viable one. Franco Moretti, an astute commentator on this tradition and its dissolution, describes the developments responsible for its undoing: "psychology started to dismantle the unified image of the individual; ... the social sciences turned to 'synchrony' and 'classification,' thereby shattering the synthetic perception of history; ... in ideology after ideology the individual figured simply as a part of the whole."[3] With the novelist's gift for personifying an abstraction, Saul Bellow describes "the oddly dispersed, ragged, mingled, broken, amorphous creature" who dominates the human landscapes of modern literature: "A cubistic, Bergsonian, uncertain, eternal, mortal someone who shuts and opens like a concertina and makes a strange music."[4]

Human character has changed, then, and hardly, it seems, for the better. Rather than being represented or experienced as a unity, novelistic character now manifests itself as a somewhat unsightly agglomeration of disparate and ill-assorted parts. Yet looked at long and closely enough, this ramshackle image of the individual begins to exert its own fascination and even its own strange appeal. True, its profile seems amorphous by conventional standards, but once our eyes adjusts to its jagged contours we begin to discern how, as in a Cubist painting, its various, apparently discontinuous aspects suddenly become visible not only in themselves but in relation to each other. Modern novelistic characters may be broken, amorphous, uncertain, and oddly dispersed, but they still feel and recognize themselves to be a mortal *someone*; they are not yet just *anyone*.

The modernist assault on individuality might have demolished the unity of character, but it could not dislodge or discredit the conviction that there is a *core* subsisting beneath all surface manifestations of character. We recognize the validity of that conviction in the modern concept of the Self, which unlike the concept of individuality, is multiform, exists both in single or plural form. It can be divided, or, to put it more positively, multiplied into separate, even rivalrous, and contending parts, without losing a sense of its own fundamental reality.

The Self is a word that has occupied a prominent place in philosophical as well as in novelistic accounts of character, but it becomes increasingly capitalized, that is, it receives a new emphasis, becomes charged with as much anxiety as prestige, after the scientific, especially the psychoanalytic and ideological critique of individuality as a fantasy of the ego or a mirage of false consciousness. The self-designated "biology watcher" Lewis Thomas was fascinated by the persistent ambiguity that hovers over a word so firmly associated with our feeling that there is, somewhere within us, something "separate from everything else, absolutely individual and independent":

> The original root was *se* or *seu*, simply the pronoun of the third person and most of the descendant words, except "self" itself, were constructed to allude to other, somehow connected people: "sibs" and "gossips," relatives and close acquaintances, come from *seu*. *Se* was also used to indicate something outside or apart, hence words like "separate," secret and segregate. From the extended root *swedh* it moved into Greek as *ethnos*, meaning people of ones own sort, and *ethos*, meaning the customs of such people. "Ethics" means the behavior of people like oneself, one's own ethnics.[5]

The modern idea of the Self, then, can claim kinship with the *ethnos* and ethics of Greek characters, with their sharply delineated features and their "ethnic" consciousness of where and with whom they belong. In its gradual but decisive evolution from a third to a first person pronoun, the Self, psychologically as well as grammatically, shed its more gregarious associations with people to whom it felt emotionally or morally connected – relatives, close acquaintances, social or ethnic kindred – and became inward and increasingly isolated from the immediate reality – but also the persuasive or coercive force – of other people.

This is indeed, where George Eliot takes up the moral history of the Self, a history she traces back to its beginnings in the instinctive, gulping narcissism of infancy. "We are all of us born in moral stupidity, taking the world as an udder to feed our supreme selves," (M, p.205). she informs us (and against us) in *Middlemarch*. That our supreme selves represent neither the highest nor the most developed part of who we are is the most obvious, but not the sole conclusion to be drawn from Eliot's dry irony. The Self of infancy, however morally stupid in thinking the world exists only to satisfy and minister to its wants, is nonetheless a centered self, indeed it is *the* center of the universe it takes to be orbiting around it. This, Emerson counters with an even more withering and compelling irony, is what at once fascinates and disconcerts us in the looks and actions of the newly born – that the infant seems to exist in untroubled accord with the deepest needs and laws of its own nature: "Infancy conforms to nobody: all conform to it, so that one babe commonly makes four or five out of the adults who prattle and play to it."[6] For Emerson, the infant is a primordial being who impresses and importunes us with its own irresistible claims, "claims not to be put by."

Eliot, for her part, is more concerned in demonstrating the moral necessity of outgrowing our infantile relationship to the world and reaching that level of maturity where we can recognize the moral reality and moral claims of other people as "equivalent centres of self" just as eager to press their importunate claims. Eliot champions the ethical vocation of the novel to educate us out of our initial moral stupidity, not by abandoning the idea of the centered Self, but by integrating it into what we might call the novelistic system of justice: a system that adjudicates and finally determines the "fair" and "right" balance of equivalences.

This is the utopian promise the novel inherits from the mythology of the Golden Age, whose principles Don Quixote recalls and expounds in his disquisition to the goatherds of the Sierra Morena, the audience economically and culturally closest to the childhood of mankind. It was an epoch that was called Golden, Don Quixote explains,

> not because gold, which in this our age of iron is so highly esteemed, could be found then with no effort, but because those who lived in that time did not know the two words *thine* and *mine* ... In that blessed age all things were owned in common; no one for his daily sustenance, needed to do more than lift his hand and pluck it from the sturdy oaks that so liberally invited to share their sweet and flavorsome fruit. (DQ, p.76, emphasis in text)

Don Quixote here elaborates a myth of Nature as the supremely good Mother, liberally bestowing her bounties on her children without their having to do more than reach out, like the infant groping at the breast, for the nourishment it craves. There is much of what Eliot calls "moral stupidity" in this vision of the world as an udder to feed our supreme selves. There is also a moral grandeur, more knowing than may first appear, in recalling a time when the world *seemed* a Golden Age in which all our needs and wants, being one, were satisfied. Envisioning the infancy of humankind as a Golden Age is a way of imagining the way the world might yet become; Eden is not only our image for a paradise lost, but also a paradise regained. So before we dismiss the infantile character of this myth, we should concede how much moral beauty is communicated through the "pretty oracles," as Emerson identifies them, of the human being and the world in its first ages.

In *Don Quixote* these oracles still speak with authority and are honored, at least by Don Quixote, as counsels of wisdom. They revive but also socialize the infant's feeling that the world and the mother's body were indistinguishably one and belonged, in a way that no subsequent possessions ever could, to oneself. Importantly, possession in this context is not burdened by distinctions of mine and thine, for the infant is as yet ignorant of such distinctions as a basis for apportioning the bounties of the world. "In that time," Don Quixote relates,

> all was peace, friendship, and harmony; the heavy curve of the plowshare had not yet dared to open or violate the merciful womb of our first mother, for she, without being forced, offered up, everywhere across her broad and fertile bosom, whatever would satisfy, sustain, and delight the children who then possessed her." (DQ, pp. 76–7)

So described, the Golden Age reveals itself as the social projection and idealization of some primal memory of the infant happily feeding at the maternal breast. Nature is a mother, the sustainer as well as giver of life, who does not recognize, much less enforce distinctions between mine and thine. Looming in the shadows of this maternal idyll is the specter of the Oedipal father, opening and violating the "merciful" womb. It is the specter of the possessive, but indisputably fecund father and his genital sexuality that startles the infant out of its dream of fertility without procreation. Men dream of the blessed age when swords will be turned into plowshares, but for the infants, remembering the bliss of possessing without penetrating the Mother, the plowshare is the instrument that, in cultivating the earth, violates it.

Me and Mine

This infant fantasy of the supreme self in its first relation to the world suggests that what the Self seeks is not happiness, but plenitude, fullness of being. The Self needs to be fed and replenished, first with bodily, then with those immaterial goods that minister to its emotional, mental and spiritual well-being. This is made humanely clear by William James in his *Principles of Psychology*. James systematically identifies and analyzes four "levels" of the Self, each with its particular, although interrelated needs: first the Empirical Self, which provides the foundation for the social and spiritual Self; at the highest level is found the Pure Ego, in which we experience, if we are capable of reaching this level of awareness, a transcendent feeling of personal unity. James sensibly begins his inquiry into the structure and character of the Self with its most "common acceptation" – that is, with the Empirical Self, which he defines in the following way: "The Empirical Self of each of us is all that he is tempted to call by the name of *me*." James immediately admits that "it is clear that between what a man calls *me* and what he simply calls *mine* the line is difficult to draw." Nonetheless, James proceeds to draw that line with admirable precision and finesse: "In its widest possible sense," James proposes (and italicizes for emphasis),

> *A man's Self is the sum total of all that he CAN call his*, not only his body and his psychic powers, but his clothes and his house, his wife and children, his ancestors and friends, his reputation and works, his lands and horses, and yacht and bank-account. All these things give him the same emotions. If they wax and prosper, he feels triumphant; if they dwindle and die away, he feels cast down – not necessarily in the same degree for each thing, but in much the same way for all.[7]

Let us sort through the tangle of feelings and possessions that make up what James contends is our most immediate and most substantial Self, the ME at the heart and center of our conscious being. What is Me is inextricably bound up with what is mine. This primal and Empirical Me is a stranger or an opponent to the ethos of the Golden Age, when possessions were shared and there was no way to designate, grammatically, psychologically, or legally, the difference between mine and thine. The Self psychologically lives in the Iron Age – the age of fathers wielding swords and plowshares to subjugate the earth and impose their wills. In this fallen but curiously advanced state of human development, who you are is determined and expressed by what you possess, not just material possessions, of course, but also the moral goods – or deficiencies – that must enter into how we account for ourselves.

This essentially novelistic conception of the Self derives from, but is not to be confused with the novelistic Individual, the free-standing subject of the first person singular. "I" is the habitual usage of Individuals, who are agents and actors, who state things about themselves and about the world; "me" is the first person pronoun of Selves, who are more likely to exchange or divide common properties, can be enriched or depleted and, unlike the Individual, who is fundamentally intact, have changeable and various social personalities. As any good dictionary might show, *Me* can grammatically and semantically occupy multiple positions. Merriam Webster's, for example, helpfully notes these various usages: "absolutely <who, *me*?>, emphatically <*me* too>, and after prepositions, conjunctions, and verbs, including *be* <come with *me*> <you're as big as *me*> <it's *me*>." Absolutely, emphatically, and inclusively, the Self is a Me that answers for who and how and even where we are.

The contention between those who conceive of character primarily in terms of an integrated and assertive I and those for whom character is more fully denoted by the things or powers it claims to possess is the subject of one of the most famous and sharp exchanges in (Henry) James's *The Portrait of a Lady*. It occurs in one of the many early conversations between Madame Merle and

Isabel Archer, and it explicitly concerns itself with the relation, such as it is, of people to the place and things that surround and are identified with them. Madame Merle admonishes Isabel for declaring that she doesn't care anything about Gilbert Osmond's house. "That's very crude of you," she at once cautions and criticizes her.

> When you've lived as long as I you'll see that every human being has his shell and that you must take the shell into account. By shell I mean the whole envelope of circumstances. There is no such thing as an isolated man or woman; we're each of us made up of some cluster of appurtenances. What shall we call our "self"? Where does it begin? Where does it end? It overflows into everything that belongs to us – and then it flows back again. I know a large part of myself is in the clothes I choose to wear. I've a great respect for *things!* One's self – for other people – is one's expression of one's self; and one's house, one's furniture, one's garments, the books one reads, the company one keeps – these things are all expressive." (PL, p.253)

At this point the narrator, perhaps worried that too much is being expressed, which in the Jamesian economy virtually means that too much is in danger of being given away, offers the helpful, if somewhat tendentious remark that "This was very metaphysical." We should be grateful for James's warning, which alerts us that we are approaching the more abstract science of being, a science in which the novel is an indefatigable researcher. Here Henry James anticipates the theory of selfhood his brother, William, will later expound in his equally arresting prose:

> The old saying that the human person is composed of three parts – soul, body and clothes – is more than a joke. We so appropriate our clothes and identify ourselves with them that there are few of us who if asked to choose between having a beautiful body clad in raiment perpetually shabby and unclean, and having an ugly and blemished form always spotlessly attired, would not hesitate a moment before making a decisive reply.[8]

James does not himself expressly give the reply, so certain is he of the answer. Beckett's spiritually immaculate tramps who pride themselves on their blemished forms, shabby attire, and general air of dilapidation would treat the question – and the old saying that inspired it – as the sublime joke it was perhaps originally intended to be. In *Sartor Resartus* Carlyle expounds on the question with all of the sublimity and none of the dark joking humor of Beckett: "Language," he famously wrote,

> is called the Garment of thought. Men are properly said to be clothed with Authority, clothed with Beauty, with Curses, and the like. Nay, if you consider it, what is Man himself, and his whole terrestrial Life, but an Emblem; a Clothing or visible Garment for that divine ME of his, cast hither, like a light-particle, down from Heaven? Thus is he said also to be clothed with a Body.[9]

This is all very metaphysical, indeed, too metaphysical even for someone as interested in the philosophy of clothes as Madame Merle. That is because, astute as she is, Madame Merle does not consider her body or her existence as the visible garment of the divine Me within her. She stakes her hope of life on the actual clothes adorning and expressing her Empirical Me.

She thus finds her moral bearings and her moral emblems elsewhere – in the idea of a Self learned from the many realistic novels I suspect her of having read and whose representations of characters in their relation to society she took to be quite reliable, even infallible guides for social, if not spiritual survival. The Self of the realistic novel is the empirical Me objectified and made visible to itself and to others through what it calls and claims as *mine*: my house, such as it is and whether owned, or rented, or merely occupied – an important and sore point for a woman like Madame Merle, who is always *visiting*, who can claim no place of her own, a dispossession that prefigures the more transcendental homelessness of Conrad's moral castaways, Hemingway's rootless émigrés, and the displaced persons and stateless wanderers in the diasporic fiction of Nabokov, Naipaul, and Sebald; my clothes, my cultural capital (books and knowledge, ideally one's possession of, or proximity to, art), my most intimate, but also my more fleeting, acquaintances – all are possessions that endow the Self with its socially visible as well as intrinsic character.

Madame Merle's psychological speculations are even more impressive than her forays into the metaphysics of character. In maintaining that the self "overflows into everything that belongs to it – and then flows back again," Madame Merle is also anticipating Freud's description of the dynamic fluidity of our mental life, which he also expresses in hydraulic terms – that is, as a libidinal Force that is constantly projected outwards, that "overflows" into the objective world of things and persons and even ideas and then, in an equally powerful and self-protective motion, returns to itself, where it is made available for other forms of expression.

In a tone that is hard to evaluate, but that certainly must influence how we are to interpret this impromptu disquisition on the Self, the narrator takes this moment to describe Madame Merle as an accomplished woman. She has not only seen the world, but acquired a knowledge of it and turned that knowledge into a "theory" of the Self that constitutes an achievement in itself. James wants to remind us of this fact about her before turning to Isabel's response. "I don't agree with you," she replies, rather calmly, I think, given this pointed challenge to the way she thinks about herself and everybody else for that matter:

> I don't know whether I succeed in expressing myself, but I know that nothing else expresses me. Nothing that belongs to me is any measure of me: everything's on the contrary a limit, a barrier, and a perfectly arbitrary one. Certainly the clothes that, as you say, I choose to wear, don't express me; and heaven forbid they should! (PL, p.253).

Isabel, who the narrator explicitly refers to in this passage as "our heroine" (as opposed to "this accomplished woman" who has befriended and will betray her), is not as loquacious as Madame Merle, in part because she has less invested in making herself clear to others. Indeed she seems to take a kind of pride in being unworried by whether she succeeds on this occasion, as on many others, in expressing herself.

Of course, this supports rather than undermines her theory that nothing, including her own words, can express her objectively. Originals have their credo, and so do Individuals, and Isabel's is as fine as we are likely to get: Individuals are so unique that they cannot be expressed by arbitrary signs; the "stuff" or core of their character can neither be contained nor limited by things, however intimately connected to them they might be. But this, too, as James might object, is getting rather metaphysical. Suffice it to say that Isabel's belief in her own individuality is trumpeted in her insistence that the clothes she wears, even those she herself has chosen, do not express her; stripped of them, she would not feel, as we suspect Madame Merle would, utterly naked. Neither garments nor language, which Carlyle defines as the garment of thought, correspond to her inner sense of who she is.

(Henry) James is less interested in resolving these differences than in keeping them in play. Still, in terms of the ideology of character, it seems to me that although Isabel, a disciple of the Individualist creed of American Transcendentalism, is the New World heroine of the piece, Madame Merle is its novelistic intelligence, albeit it in its most worldly – or its most despairing? – form. For it is Madame Merle who sees her "Self" expressed by the whole "envelope" of material and social circumstances in which she may, at any given moment, find herself enclosed. It is Madame Merle who links the life of the Self with its ability to be seen – and who, consequently, appreciates what it might mean to be invisible.

Visualizing the Self

By 1925, the year Virginia Woolf's *Mrs Dalloway* was published and well after human character had changed, the argument still has not been resolved, but it has visibly shifted. For one thing, the argument has been internalized as an inner dialogue modern characters routinely have with themselves. Certainly the conversation Mrs Dalloway has with herself may be said to constitute one of the central, ongoing actions of the novel bearing her name, a novel, moreover, whose final sentence – "For there she was" – suggests that her character can only be manifested, never definitively expressed. We never doubt that Emma Woodhouse is handsome, clever, and rich and that her actions logically and morally follow from the physical, mental and social endowments that define her. Mrs Dalloway, on the contrary, begins her day insisting "that she would not say of herself, I am this, I am that."[10] It is a conviction in line with Isabel Archer's feeling that nothing definitely expresses her, that her inner being cannot be located, confined, or reduced to a "this" or a "that." Mrs Dalloway has, as we shall see, certain personality traits, mental habits, and social standing, but unlike Emma, these attributes do not coalesce to form an individual "character." The outlines of her character are indefinite and irregular and sometimes scarcely discernible.

We see how her sense of herself as resistant to definition at first cheers, then begins to unsettle her as she makes her way down Bond Street. In the open air and among a throng of people unknown to her, she feels herself become attenuated into a pitiably hollow "shell" that has lost the luster as well as the density of self-presence. Without an enlivening sense of the Me and mine – those traits, memories, relationships, and most especially the body that belong to and express her Self – she feels invisible not only to others but, more tellingly, to herself.

> She had the oddest sense of being herself invisible, unseen; unknown; there being no more marrying, no more having of children now, but only this astonishing and rather solemn progress with the rest of them, up Bond Street, this being Mrs. Dalloway; not even Clarissa any more; this being Mrs. Richard Dalloway. (MD, p.11)

The difference between Mrs Dalloway, the title character whose name inaugurates the novel, almost with the force of an invocation, and the Mrs Dalloway who feels herself invisible, unseen, and unknown as she parades down Bond Street is indicated by the effacement, however temporary, of her personal name. The personal name is one of the first and most valuable properties the Self acquires and its loss can distress, even devastate the Empirical Me. But it can also incite the Self to seek out new moral properties. Ellison's Invisible Man has no name at all, but then neither does the narrator of Proust's epic of recollection, *Remembrance of Things Past*. The monumental task of both these Self-seeking narrators is to find the matter to substantiate and "fill out" their Self, their "Empirical Me." The books they write tell how they came into possession of themselves.

Mrs Dalloway, of course, is not the narrator of her own life, although she is a fairly astute commentator upon it. Proust's and Ellison's narrators remain nameless, in part because as male narrators their relation to their name is not, to the degree it is with women who marry, mediated by social convention. This substitution of Richard's name where her own might reasonably appear is one of the many small, but effective ways in which Woolf realizes her desire to "criticize the social system & show it at work at its most intense."[11] For a name is one of the most psychologically valuable as well as socially prized possessions in the "cluster of appurtenances" that express and identify the empirical Me. (The social Me is identified by a first and last name, and all the titles and honorifics attached to it that indicate status – married, credentialed, of aristocratic or royal lineage.) Women, apparently, are as much in danger of relinquishing their personal as their last name under patriarchy. They also are vulnerable to even greater confiscations of those social appurtenances that express the Self and give it a certain standing in the world. Although Woolf is not as rabid a believer in an embodied Selfhood as Madame Merle, she has a deeper and ultimately a more mystical sense of what it would be like to be completely without one.

Woolf, however, eases this concern almost as soon as she raises it. For as the novel makes perfectly and almost immediately clear, Clarissa, the name by which Clarissa is known to herself as well as to her family and friends, has not been erased, only held in suspension until the Self who corresponds and answers to that name is summoned. Woolf describes this act of self-recall and reconsolidation in quasi-ritualistic terms: "There is an emptiness at the heart of life, an attic room," Clarissa thinks on returning home. "Women must put off their rich apparel. At midday they must disrobe." Once divested of the garments that cover not only her own essential nakedness, but that of Life itself, she sits before her mirror, where she, so conscious of how she appears to others, is now visible to herself:

> How many million times she had seen her face, and always with the same imperceptible contraction! She pursed her lips when she looked in the glass. It was to give her face point. That was her self – pointed; dartlike; definite. That was herself when some effort, some call on her to be her self, drew the parts together, she alone knew how different, how incompatible and composed so for the world only into one centre, one diamond, one woman who sat in her drawing-room and made a meeting point, a radiancy no doubt in some dull lives: a refuge for the lonely to come to perhaps; (MD, p.40)

Mirrors are conventional, but notoriously unreliable mediums of self-reflection. The face that looks back at us in the mirror can as easily leave us with a feeling of estrangement – is that really my bodily, Empirical Me? – as of recognition – Yes, that's me all right. The face that greets Clarissa in her mirror is a familiar one, but the exclamation point that punctuates this moment injects a note of comic exasperation into this otherwise solemn ritual of self-recognition. The exasperation is provoked not only by what she sees, but how she comes to see it: through the same imperceptible, but tell-tale contraction that signals the continuity of herself – or at least of her mirrored image – over time. Clarissa is aware, as few novelistic characters were before her, of a bodily ego whose reflexes are more indicative of who she is than her vagrant thoughts and changeable feelings. Who wouldn't be chagrined to discover that a reflex, a muscular rather than a spiritual movement, is a more reliable expression of what is most constant in our character?

This impression persists only as long as we believe that the mirror before her is reflecting "her self" as she "really" is; but this proves not to be the case. The Self who answers to Clarissa's deepest understanding of who she is does not "naturally" appear, but is summoned by a practiced act of the mind. Looking at the face that belongs exclusively to her is not sufficient to give Clarissa a sense of her empirical, much less her essential, innermost, inviolable Me. She must physically conjure "her self" by pursing her lips, inducing the contraction that will give her face a point, for that is the way she sees herself – pointed; dartlike; definite. Yet no sooner is the point made than it begins to lose its definiteness and dissolve into a palpable, but immaterial radiance. Even when she is alone, facing herself, Clarissa apparently has trouble keeping to the point. She moves from the point that is her Self to the meeting-point she is for other people. It is almost as if her Self must be centered not as a matter of moral and psychological necessity, but as a social obligation. In the quasi-sacramental language this ritual moment seems to require, we could say that Clarissa's self-composure before her mirror is the visible sign of a social grace that she regards almost in the light of a spiritual and existential one. Clarissa may bristle at hearing her former suitor, Peter Walsh, brand her "a perfect hostess," but that is the ego-ideal she has, in fact, internalized.

Mrs Dalloway is hardly the first, nor will she be the last fictional heroine to sit before her mirror and to be confounded, even chagrined by what she sees reflected there. But she is among the first modern characters to confront the *antithetical* nature of the Self as both deeply personal and profoundly social. This deep identity cannot be adduced to some trick or disorder of the mind. It represents an authentic discovery about how the Self is emotionally and psychologically organized. With his customary lucidity, William James explains and extols the paradox by which our innermost, most intimate, and most centered sense of who we are turns out to be "a Self of the *social* sort"(James's emphasis).[12] Not just any sort, James is quick to add, but an ideal social sort on whom we project the moral and spiritual values we like to think we represent. Thus it is, James remarks, that this ideal social Self that comes to stand for "the true, the intimate, the ultimate, the permanent Me which I seek."[13]

We are now in a better position to appreciate Lewis Thomas's insistence on the ambiguities and contradictions encompassed by the word Self. It can designate the most intimate and independent and at the same time the most social aspects of our character. In its disposition to contain and convey antithetical meanings, the Self should be considered a primal word in the sense that Freud defined it – a word that unites two antithetical ideas or meanings as different aspects of the same reality. (The essay in which Freud explored the meanings of primal words and their connection to the dream work, "The Antithetical Meaning of Primal Words," was published in 1910, another sign that human character, or certainly our perception of it, had changed.[14]) If Woolf occupies such a central place in this discussion of modern selfhood and its vicissitudes, it is because among modern novelists, she has the most highly developed antithetical sense of the Self as a primal word. In *Mrs Dalloway* the antithetical character of the Self is expressed through the image of the point as both a point of self-consolidation, where all the different and often incompatible parts of the inner Self converge, and simultaneously a meeting-point where the Self becomes visible and available to others.

Woolf would in fact relentlessly experiment with forms that would test the density and sturdiness of that point on which, at any given moment, Selfhood is so precariously poised. She was psychologically aware, as perhaps no other modern novelist was, that a point is not a stable thing, but a place, a marker of position. Her novels track the flow of consciousness as it moves toward or away from this point that marks both the center and circumference of the innermost Self. These movements, when plotted, themselves point in two antithetical directions. One comprises a movement into the most private recesses of the mind, where the light of the world seldom penetrates and where, Woolf speculates in *Orlando*, "everything is reflected." She remarks, almost too casually given the staggering implications of her claims, that "indeed, some say that all our most violent passions, and art and religion are the reflections which we see in the dark hollow at the back of the head when the visible world is obscured for a time."[15] Beckett's Murphy pictures his mind in strikingly similar terms as a "large hollow sphere, hermetically closed to the universe without" (Murphy, p.107). For both Woolf and Beckett, hollowness does not signify emptiness, the impoverishment of the solitary consciousness.[16] Quite the opposite. If character wants room, it will find space aplenty in the hollows at the back of the mind. Here the Self is as full as it can ever hope to become: everything in the world is reflected and contained within it. The modern novel is notable for its fascination with interiors, but of all interiors, the mind is the most spacious and the most richly furnished. Sadly, the reverse is also true. In times of psychological and economic depression, the large hollow at the back of the head may seem cavernous, a void incapable of being filled; it is then the mind feels itself unbearably empty and, consequently, most bereft.

But even the most determined solipsist, like Murphy, cannot remain permanently ensconced in the mind's copious darkness. The novel pitilessly insists on returning them to the daylight realm of physical experience, of human interchange, of moral exertion. The hollow at the back of the head may include "everything" outside the mind, everything, that is, except the reflections stored in the back of other heads. Even the novel's Originals had to acknowledge and contend with the reality of other characters, who may not have been as imaginative or generous or handsome or clever or rich, but who nonetheless refused to relinquish their rights as independent centers of life, hence of human significance. In the modern novel, the Self which commands the hollow space of the back of the head is finally given its rightful place in the novelistic account of human character. Yet if we are truthful, and the best novelists always are, this Self cannot justly represent and motivate us in our dealings with other people. For this, we return to and rely on the Empirical, Visible, Sociable Me who gives us our distinct identity and place in the world.

All in All

Still, the Empirical Self, being acquisitive and never feeling complete (or complete enough!), still strives for those states in which everything seems within its reach. The modern novel, as the chronicler of the Self's search for plenitude, takes us not only underneath and within, but also beyond the visible surface the Empirical Self shows to the world. For there are indeed moments when the Self wants to be taken out of itself, when it yearns to venture beyond the mental and linguistic perimeters of its entrenched and centered selfhood. It feels a need to find new social forms that will extend and enrich it. Woolf envisioned one such form in the writing of *The Years*, a novel whose focus would not be on the Empirical Me, but on the grammatical and existential vagaries of a narrative "We." This "We" was to be composed of many different things ... all life, all art, all waifs and strays – a rambling capacious but somehow unified whole – the present state of my mind?"[17] Whether traveling inward or reaching outward, the Self wants and is ready to receive *everything*, even the waifs and strays that in more prudent or stinting moods it would reject as so many unassimilable and wayward oddities disruptive to its inner unity and calm. Woolf imagines, both as a blessing and a perplexity, a future point at which the Self might be stretched to its limits in trying to accommodate "all life, all art." Here is further evidence of the Self's desire for plenitude, for fullness of being. Both the route inward and the extension outward ideally culminate in that point where the Self experiences itself as Unity in which everything is reflected and all life and art are included. What a point this would be, could we but reach it!

Few, of course, reach that point, fewer still can remain there. The artist is a particular exception to this general rule. If the artistic character comes to dominate the modern fictions of Selfhood, it is because the artist can boast a more inclusive and morally significant relation to multifarious Life than the traditional heroes or heroines of the novel, who are constrained by their distinct personalities. This is the boast that sounds through Stephen Dedalus's imaginative biography of Shakespeare, the intellectual centerpiece and artistic manifesto at the center of Joyce's *Ulysses*. In the face of considerable skepticism, outright mockery, and his own considerable self-doubts, Stephen argues that Shakespeare could embody the infinite variety of the world because he was "All in all": "In *Cymbeline*, in *Othello*, he is bawd and cuckold. He acts and is acted on. Lover of an ideal and a perversion, like José he kills the real Carmen. His unremitting intellect is the hornmad Iago ceaselessly willing that the moor in him shall suffer."[18] Stephen depicts Shakespeare's creative Self not as containing everything but of being everyone, an important and definitive difference. He also portrays him as the consummate antithetical Self: agent and victim, lover of ideals and the perversions that mock and degrade them, ardent rationalist and insane sower of doubt and destruction. The artist began to emerge as a figure of novelistic interest, even anxiety, only when prose fiction began to represent the antithetical, multiple, indeed multipointed character of the Self. Once the artist could be acknowledged as the highest and most inclusive form of character, then characters, even those without specific vocations, could be esteemed for their artistic as much as their moral proclivities: even his disparagers don't dispute that there is a bit of the artist in old Bloom; Mrs Ramsay, the managing, sometimes interfering maternal presence irradiating *To the Lighthouse,* is credited by Lily Briscoe, herself a painter, with having mastered the art of life.

Artists are artists because they can objectify the active and passive, aggressive and timid, loving and lascivious, supremely rational or cunningly insane selves that inhabit the hollow at the back of their brain. But there are other more immaterial but equally sublime ways to feel, even if one cannot claim to be, All in All. These are the feelings mystics report upon their transumption into some greater Totality. The modern novelist is interested in such states because they represent another way the Self might organize and orient itself in its relation to other people and to Reality in all its transcendent splendor. Kenneth Burke proposes that the mystic self represents "the verbal equivalent of a universalized first person pronoun," a kind of "super-person envisaged beyond language but through language" who may be considered as "generically human rather than individually human."[19]

The novel can gesture toward this generic rather than individualized Self, purged of all the pride and burden of its possessions, all its sociality, all its strivings after perfection, but it cannot accommodate it any more than it could give permanent home to the innermost and invisible Self who occupies the back of the brain. For the novel, as I hope to have established by now, is where distinctive character asserts and defends itself, makes, when necessary, its stand against the forces that would tamper, deform, absorb, or extinguish its singular existence. Thus even as Woolf contemplates writing a fiction in which the self-centered "I" will be replaced by an all-inclusive and encompassing "We," she returns to her starting point – the empirical Me that represents, at any given moment, "the present state of my mind."

We might deduce from the inevitability of this return one of the foundational laws of the novel: that the spiritual and not just the material world of the novel is subject to the law of gravity. Everything that rises may converge, but sooner or later even the most soaring spirits must come back to earth and take up their grounded and particularized existence. Kipling at once defies and enforces this law in plotting the fate of his characters in *Kim*. The novel begins in the rousing mode of an adventure-spy tale but almost immediately metamorphoses, without loss of energy or excitement, into a quest narrative that seamlessly coordinates Kim's skillful maneuvers as a vital player of the Great Game between Russian and British imperial interests in Central Asia with his attentive service to his newly acquired spiritual Teacher, a Tibetan lama on a pilgrimage "to free [himself] from the Wheel of Things by a great and open road."[20] At novel's end, we know that the Great Game will continue, with different players, into the indefinite future. Indeed it is being played by other players with savage and desperate intensity as I write. Nor can the spiritual quest be said to have been concluded, even though the Teshhoo Lama reports that he had in fact reached the threshold of freedom where he was "loosed from the silly body" and was on the brink of entering into the "Great Soul which is beyond all things."

This spiritual summit becomes the vantage point from which he claims to have seen not only the Causes of Things, but their earthly incarnations: "all Hind," every stage of his journey, the body of Kim grappling with an idolater, and his own "stupid body lying down." Kipling renders this dream-vision as a kind of metaphysical comedy that combines piety, tenderness, and humor to bring about a spiritual Deliverance in which the Self becomes at once more and less than itself. The comedy ends, as comedies generally do, with the sanctified image of a couple, in this instance the "beloved" pairing of the master and disciple, the Teshoo Lama and Kim, the Son of his Soul, whose Deliverance he declares to be both imminent and certain. The final human utterance of the novel is "Come," an invitation to Kim – and presumably to those readers predisposed to such spiritual adventures – to follow the spiritual itinerary that leads to the Great Soul beyond all things. But the novel itself cannot follow him there, if it wants to remain a novel. It must remain bound to the Wheel of Things and the embodied Life of the World.

This E. M. Forster was to discover in the writing of *A Passage to India*, when, responding to the same "call" India issues to the spirit, he found himself unable to answer in the way he had hoped. "Except" is the first word of the novel, and though it is used to describe the unusual and disorientating configurations of the Marabar Caves, it soon gravitates to the character of Mrs Moore, the novel's unlikely elderly heroine, whose capacity for unforced sympathy and her easy disregard of the hierarchal protocols that define life in Anglo-India promises to – and in many significant ways *does* – take the novel into spiritual territories that exist, in Forster's words "beyond the educated vision."[21] Her very name is a Dickensian sign that her mission is to supplement the novel's conventional assortment of characters: the well-meaning Fielding, the earnest Adela Quested, the sympathetic Aziz, the coy but genuinely mysterious Godbole, and the foolish and officious, but powerful community of Anglos who administer colonial rule. None of these characters, even the most creditable or endearing, like Fielding and Aziz, can or will depart from their assigned character. More importantly, none of them, except the Hindu priest Godbole, can introduce anything *else* into the cultural comedy of manners in which they play so important, if reluctant a part.

Mrs Moore can move the novel into exceptional directions precisely because, as a character, she has already experienced the "all in all" the traditional novel had to offer in the way of human experience. Her advanced age gives her a special authority in evaluating and often dispensing with the human traditions and feelings that have been the main preoccupations of the traditional novel – with marriage, for example, as a human as well as social good. Feeling that "people are important, but the relations between them are not" (PI, p.156), she understandably has difficulty sticking to "the real serious subject" that brought her to India – whether her son should marry – and finds that she is increasingly preoccupied instead with thoughts of God. These thoughts are unpretentiously ecumenical: she removes her shoes when entering a mosque even when no one is looking because for her "God is here;" later she addresses a wasp that has strayed into her bedroom as "pretty dear," as if in spiritual greeting. All these small, but morally resonant departures from the conventions and protocols that regulate her social and even her spiritual life feed our hope that she will bring something exceptional to the novel's acerbic comedy of multicultural manners and its creditable but hardly remarkable Liberal indictment of colonialist rule.

She does, but hardly in the positive way that the novel initially leads us to expect. Even as the novel looks more and more to Mrs Moore to articulate a new novelistic ethos for the Self, it refuses to decide whether Mrs Moore's vagrant thoughts and wayward intimations of spiritual realities that remain unknown or unacknowledged by the rationalist, empirical Western ego, represent a vision or nightmare. The question is decided, however, once and for all, in the climactic and scandalous incident of the Marabar Caves, in which nothing and everything seems to happen. Mrs Moore enters a cave, carrying all the novel's hopes for an exceptional glimpse into a Reality that has eluded the clear-eyed, Apollonian gaze of the Western eye. She comes out as a character reverting to, and yet insufficiently consoled or even supported by, the very habits of mind and feeling she had begun to shed in her slow metamorphosis into an "Oriental." Although asked to enter another of the seemingly identical and indistinguishable caves, she refuses and insists on being left alone to contemplate the unspeakable horror that has overtaken her:

> The crush and the smells she could forget, but they began in some indescribable way to undermine her hold on life. Coming at a moment when she chanced to be fatigued, it managed to murmur, pathos, piety, courage, they exist, but are identical. Everything exists, nothing has value. If one had spoken vileness in that place, or quoted lofty poetry, the comment would have been the same, ou-boum. (PI, p.165)

Mrs Moore in particular complains of an "echo devoid of all distinction." One can understand why. The echo is at once hollow and full of everything: this "boum" is a primal word and a booming primal pun. It is the All in All from which all language emanates and to which it is fated to return. Such a word sounds incomprehensibly on the Western ear, educated in the rather different music of discriminated, articulated sounds. In the "twilight of the double vision" that undermines Mrs Moore's hold on life, Forster contemplates what it would be like to see oneself as a creature without distinction in a world that recognizes no distinctions, even the most simple moral differences between good and evil. Such a world, as Kenneth Burke reminds us, would happily be without those "picturesque stupidities rooted in hierarchal motives that come to completion in the ills of empire."[22] But he wonders whether he would be morally as well as psychologically equal to it.

Mrs Moore is certainly not up to it. She abandons the novel at the point of crisis, retreating into silence and slipping quietly away into death. But her name is taken up and translated into the minds of the Indians as Emiss Moore and becomes a rallying cry of the Indians protesting the oppressive, blundering Anglo rulers. Her linguistic apotheosis is Forster's most inspired attempt at metaphysical comedy. But he cannot sustain it anymore than Kipling could. Still, where Kipling concludes *Kim* with a smile suggesting the comedy will soon resume, Forster, the more searching novelist, ends *A Passage to India* with a rebuff to any such initiatives. These were the prospects that initially gave the novel its sense of hope, even excitement as it set out to bridge the antithetical worlds – and opposing characters – of

Occidental and Oriental, of social and visionary life, of personal relations and socio-political institutions. The collapse of these hopes is connected to the collapse of Mrs Moore in the Marabar Caves, a spiritual failure that even her translation into a minor Hindu divinity cannot reverse or compensate for. The novel ends the only way it honestly can: with an affectionate embrace between the novel's exceptional couple, Fielding and Aziz, broken up by the unaccommodating landscape of India, home to irresolvable contradictions, clamoring multitudes, and unromantic mysteries.

The Final Me

Only D. H. Lawrence, a high and late romantic in an age that looked with suspicion on untrammeled individualism, especially in its visionary moods, persisted in his struggle to find the Ultimate and Distinctive Self that could survive any spiritual challenges put to it. Given the rhetorical fury and exasperated invective of his later fiction, it is somewhat of a shock to return to his first great work, *Sons and Lovers,* and see how dispassionately, even calmly he reports the growing discrepancy between the life one lives and the person one feels oneself to be: "Sometimes life takes hold of one, carries the body along, accomplishes one's history and yet is not real, but leaves oneself as it were slurred over." The measured yet unstoppable cadences of this sentence seem themselves caught up in the same resistless forces that leave the Self a helpless bystander in the making – or unmaking – of its own life. The word "slurred" returns the focus, however, to the pathos of character striving for distinction. It also isolates the problem of self-fulfillment as a problem of self-articulation. Mrs Morel, the character who inspires these reflections, shows just how vivid a character she is, despite being slurred over by the circumstances of her life, in her lucid and articulate complaint: "I wait," Mrs Morel said to herself – "I wait, and what I wait for can never come."[23]

Lawrence was determined to bring an end to this waiting. Indignant at the human debacle of modern life, he prophesized a future populated by "wonderful distinct individuals, like angels ... each one being himself, perfect as a complete melody or a pure colour."[24] No writer ever put more demands on the Self – or on his readers – than Lawrence did in dreaming such dreams of a humanity not just refined, but perfected and purified. He was conscious of the demands and knew it would take a new conception of the novelistic Self to fulfill them. This, as he wrote to his publisher David Garnett, was his own accomplishment in *Women in Love*. "You mustn't look in my novel for the old stable *ego* of the character," he wrote.

> There is another *ego*, according to whose action the individual is unrecognizable, and passes through, as it were, allotropic states which it needs a deeper sense that any we've been used to exercise, to discover are states of the same single radically unchanged element. (Like as diamond and coal are the same pure single element of carbon. The ordinary novel would trace the history of the diamond – but I say 'diamond, what! This is carbon.' And my diamond might be coal or soot, and my theme is carbon.)[25]

Lawrence's theme may be carbon, but even Lawrence knew and appreciated the difference between diamond and soot. As he himself might put it, he had the *predilection d'artiste* for Nature's aristocrat, "the man of distinct being, who must act in his own particular way to fulfill his own individual nature." Thus the seemingly objective scientism he brought to the novel's study of character development had little in common with Darwinian theories of selection and adaptation, even less with any ideological program of political, social, and moral reform. For Lawrence, the novel might begin as a study of carbon, but it inevitably developed into the prophetic testing ground for his own natural religion. He preached the gospel of "the God-mystery within us" which sends forth "promptings of desire and aspiration,"[26] urging us to renounce the false gods of Mechanism and Money and invent new ways of living more befitting our angelic nature.

Such promptings provoke Rupert Birkin, the prophetic consciousness of *Women in Love*, to abandon the established grammar of being as obsolete to the new importunate realities germinating within him. In place of the "dead" letter "I," the "old formula of the ego," he envisions a fully realized and ultimately inhuman – or suprahuman – form of first personhood that he calls "the final me." We learn how and where we might attain this "final me" and what new way of being it offers us in the strangest declaration of love a man ever made or a woman ever received:

> "There is," he said, in a voice of pure abstraction, "a final me which is stark and impersonal and beyond responsibility. So there is a final you. And it is there I would want to meet you – not in the emotional, loving plane – but there beyond, where there is no speech and no terms of agreement. There we are two stark, unknown beings, two utterly strange creatures, I would want to approach you, and you me.– And there could be no obligation, because there is no standard for action there, because no understanding has been reaped from that plane. It is quite inhuman, – so there can be no calling to book, in any form whatsoever – because one is outside the pale of all that is accepted, and nothing known applies. One can only follow the impulse, taking that which lies in front, and responsible for nothing, asked for nothing, giving nothing, only each taking according to the primal desire." (WL, p.146)

Lawrence's mystic yearning to surpass the old novelistic ego takes him to a realm of being the novel has never visited and, indeed, might never had even suspected was there. In passages like these – and they become more numerous and more urgent as the novel, indeed as Lawrence's career, progresses – Lawrence conducts us to the threshold where the novelistic ego is purged of all the pride and burden of its possessions, all its sociality, indeed its very humanity and becomes a kind of supra-character trusting to its own pure and inerrant desires.

If this description of the transfigured self remains vague, it is because this Final Me remains unfinalized, is subject to contradictory impulses and strivings: it is at once impersonal and inhuman, yet individually distinct and self-impelled; it is bound by no standard of action and yet, in its dealings with others, is enjoined not to ask or give, but only take. Every new vision of the Self, as we saw in Forster, involves a new ethics, even if it takes the form of living outside and beyond every known and authorized feeling of responsibility or obligation. Lawrence's morality is comprehended in one positive rather than prohibitive commandment: Thou shall act according to the promptings of primal desire. To this moral imperative Lawrence attaches, however, an important corollary and stricture: "for special natures you must give a special world" (WL, p.205). Here is the one instance in which Lawrence allows that it is better to give than to take, but the odd locution – to give a special world – highlights how exceptional a provision this is. It is a provision made on behalf of special natures not yet capable of making their own world. There is no way to give such beings a special world, of course, except through the offices of imagination. This special world is the world of the novel transfigured by, but never itself transformed *into* myth.

Lawrence's pursuit of new modes of being was a Quixotic enterprise, but also venturesome and expansive as only the Quixotic spirit can be. The novel not only tolerates this spirit, but cannot exist and perpetuate itself without it. Magnanimity, the moral energy dedicated to the increase and enhancement of life, is as much the ultimate novelistic, as it is the primary Quixotic virtue. James Joyce is another novelist who writes in this magnanimous spirit, although his generosity is of another and arguably of a more welcome sort. (I know few contemporary readers who respond to Lawrence's prophecies with gratitude.) As we might expect from an artist who aspired to be, like Shakespeare, All in All, Joyce devised a myth of Self that contained rather than surpassed the world. Both Lawrence and Joyce elevate self-seeking into an epic quest, but whereas Lawrence relentlessly, even pitilessly sheds all attachments to the world as it is, Joyce works tirelessly to note, inventory, enclose, contain, and transfigure (ideally to ennoble – this is after all a Quixotic ambition) Reality in all its vivid particulars. He thus strikes us as the more inclusive and sympathetic, although finally the less adventurous writer, for however far the Joycean character may travel, he always finds his way home. For Joyce, *nostos* or homecoming, the return and ingathering of the outgoing and dispersed Self, is the mythic destination of all human wandering. Lawrence's visionary wanderers never find a permanent place to settle; for them return to "the actual world" is never to be thought of.

As *Ulysses* ingeniously illustrates, Joyce, in voluntary and permanent exile himself, has the *predilection d'artiste* for the homebound character, with all the ambiguities entailed by that word bound. Stephen, the vagrant artist and centrifugal departer who is yet to find his "final me," is the novel's free radical, unbound and unpaired. Despite his intelligence, he is unreliable as an example and model of substantial, morally lovable, self-accepting, and self-validating character. One reason that Stephen, whose consciousness dominates the *Telemachiad*, the first three chapters of *Ulysses*, is so obsessed with the nature and fate of the physical body, is that his own life, experientially and artistically, is still embryonic, lacking inner substance as well as outer bulk. Plumpness belongs to the usurpers, like Buck Mulligan, or the well-fed priestly cast whose sodality Stephen has proudly rejected. These are figures very much at ease in the world, equipped with the shock absorbers of ample flesh and regular meals. Stephen, by contrast, is very much a hero in the making, a body that needs to be plumped up. There seems little hope of this, given his chronic destitution, but also because of his tendency to regard the body itself as so much carrion, fodder for the predations of time. At the conclusion of the *Telemachiad*, Stephen, for whom the world has become a Universe of Death, imagines himself as ingesting the dead forms and decayed remains of all that once lived but is no longer alive: "Dead breath I living breath; tread dead dust, devour ruinous offal from all the dead"(U, p.42). The ill-clad, ill-fed, yet still robust artificer of *Portrait* eager to forge the conscience of his race now sees himself as devourer of offal, a scavenger or carrion bird.

Joyce recalls the whiff of ruinous offal that offends and nauseates Stephen in the opening paragraph of "Calypso," where it is sublimated into the fine tang of mutton kidney lingering on Bloom's palate. Indeed Bloom's remarkable appetite for entrails is the first thing Joyce sees fit to tell us about him. He is not just a consumer, but an avid ingester of the inner organs of beasts and fowls. This hero of appetite recommends himself to an age struggling, like Stephen, with the feeling that its Empirical Me is lacking in the energy and in the substance that are essential to its moral well-being. It is in this capacity as a consumer, but also as a dispenser of life's primary commodities that the novel and this chapter first finds him – setting out a bowl of milk for the household cat whose "lithe form" he "kindly, curiously" observes. In this homely gesture and the attentive, considerate manner in which it is performed, Joyce translates, in his own idiomatic key, Quixotic magnanimity into the domain and practices of everyday life. Curiosity – the enlivening and active interest in the existence of all living, indeed all created things – and Kindness – a solicitude for their well being – are the touchstones of Joyce's ethical universe.

These extensions and identifications across the barriers of consciousness and even species form the basis of the moral and artistic economy of magnanimity that governs *Ulysses* in particular and, I would argue, the novel in general. In the lines Stephen Dedalus inscribes in the flyleaf of his geography book, Joyce suggests that the impulse of individual consciousness to extend itself into the living world is instinctive in the artist:

> Stephen Dedalus
> Class of Elements
> Clongowes Wood College
> Sallins
> County Kildare
> Ireland
> Europe
> The World
> The Universe[27]

Stephen envisions himself as a soaring individuality ascending through the levels of Creation until he attains that summit at which Self and Universe fatefully coincide. But he, like Icarus, keeps falling back to earth, collapsing back unto his self and, increasingly, into a brooding and often abject solitude.

That is where we find him at the beginning of *Ulysses*, a grounded but now decentered Self who requires a new paradigm of self-extension and self-realization. He finds it in the narrative and language of encounter (the inaugural word of Joyce's short story collection, *Dubliners*). "Every life," Stephen proclaims in one of his most positive assertions, "is many days, day after day. We walk through ourselves, meeting robbers, ghosts, giants, old men, young men, wives, widows, brothers-in-love, but always meeting ourselves" (U, p.175). In such meetings, the Self finds "in the world without as actual what was within our world as possible." No attempt to avoid or flee these encounters can keep us from becoming who we are, in Stephen's words, "ineluctably preconditioned to become" (U, p.412). Joycean characters may change their name, their appearance, their clothes, even their address (as Stephen presumably does at the novel's end), but these metamorphoses never denature them. For Joyce, mythic character (Bloom as Odysseus, Stephen as Hamlet or Shakespeare or alternately/simultaneously both, Molly as Penelope) is the genotype that is only visible through its individual incarnations. Metamorphosis in Joyce is epigenetic – the genotype may migrate from form to form, body to body, but the distinctive DNA of character remains intact. Bloom may be the modern incarnation of Odysseus, but he is nonetheless and ineluctably Bloom of 7 Eccles Street living in Dublin in 1904.

The end of Bloom's odyssey is a portent and a kind of pledge that the regenerative cycles that govern all living things in their distinct as well as generic/genetic character will continue to work their daily miracles. At the close of his epic day, Bloom enters the metamorphic realms of sleep in "the attitude depicted in a snapshot photograph made by Percy Apjohn, the childman weary, the manchild in the womb" (U, p.606). Let us inspect a bit more closely the image indistinctly but visibly projected in this sonogram. It is an image necessarily blurred by the uterine waters that surround, buoy, and nourish it. Still we can detect its genotype: the manchild and childman, ultimate as well as initial image of the Antithetical Self, awaiting its impending and ineluctable incarnation. What individual form this new incarnation might take is left undetermined, but we may reasonably wonder if it may be the product of some new ethnic and cultural combination. Odyssean Bloom is a greekjew who matures into the jewgreek. The ethnic self he ineluctably is preconditioned to become offers itself as both a genotype and forerunner of a new breed of novelistic characters who see themselves as Identities rather than Individuals or Selves.

Identities

The root of "identity" is "idem" – the same. Both in common and fictional parlance, identity refers to what appears to us to be constant and persistent, despite the changes time and experience work on our bodies, our moods and feelings, our behavior, our morals, our ideas, our loyalties, and affections. Often Self and Identity are used interchangeably, although the Self still claims the role, one could say honor, of representing our innermost sense of who we are and what we are preconditioned ineluctably to become. This sense of personal identity is often complemented, at other times usurped by a group identity, in which distinctive personal traits tend to be slurred over or obscured by more visible sexual, racial, ethnic, cultural, or national characteristics. It is precisely for this reason that I will have little specific to say about different group identities beyond remarking their power to shape and impinge on personal identity.

Identity has come to displace Self in an age and in a culture that has become increasingly multi-cultural, multi-ethnic, cosmopolitan, and multinational. Woolf had imaged the meeting point where the Self encounters and interacts with other selves as a drawing room – hence the importance of Mrs Dalloway's party as a place where the Self is made visible to others. But a self that is more aware of its outward rather than inward determinations may envision its contacts with others somewhat more anxiously – or aggressively, as the case may be. Stevenson projected the internally divided and besieged Identity as a "fortress" where our most cherished and enduring sense of who we are is lodged and defended.

The image is resonant in suggesting how character, represented as an Identity, can feel embattled, under siege, in crisis. Eric Erikson, the American social psychologist who invented the term Identity crisis, stipulated that he was using the word crisis not in the sense of "an impending catastrophe" but rather to suggest "a critical turning point, a crucial moment, when development must move one way or another marshalling resources of growth, recovery and further differentiation."[28] This account assumes, of course, a generally successful and happy outcome of such developmental crises. Yet some of Erikson's most suggestive observations on identity formation concern the more baleful and even sinister ways Identity differentiates and asserts itself. Positing that "man's need for a psychosocial identity is anchored in nothing less than his sociogenetic evolution," Erikson maintains that individual development takes place within a defined group Identity. He calls these social constellations *pseudospecies* and hypothesizes their origin and "rise" in the following terms:

> First each horde or tribe, class and nation, but then also every religious association has become *the* human species, considering all the others a freakish and gratuitous invention of some irrelevant deity. To reinforce the illusion of being chosen, every tribe recognizes a creation of its own, a mythology and later a history; thus was loyalty to a particular ecology and morality secured. One never quite knew how all the other tribes came to be, but since they did exist, they were at least useful as a screen of projection for the negative identities which were the necessary, if most uncomfortable counterpart of the positive ones.[29]

It is primarily as a *pseudospecies*, with all its defensive and bellicose impulses, that Identity attracts novelistic scrutiny. Erikson himself remarks that the increased differentiation of the social body into *psuedospecies* may explain why "revolutionary writers and writers from national and ethnic minority groups (like the Irish expatriates or our Negro and Jewish writers) have become the artistic spokesmen and prophets of identity confusion." Artists, he speculates, are willing to endure "a certain painful identity-consciousness … in order to provide the conscience of man with a critique of conditions, with the insight and the conceptions necessary to heal himself of what most deeply divides and threatens him, namely, his division in what we have called pseudospecies."[30]

The limitations and perniciousness of Identity as the basis of a *politics* originate in this disposition of *pseudospecies* to stigmatize or be stigmatized as the very condition of their social visibility. This is the great theme of Ralph Ellison's *Invisible Man*, whose nameless protagonist is a blank screen for the projection of a succession of geographically and culturally distinct Afro-American identities: Southern Negro, Urban black proletariat, communist – international brotherhood. Everything can and is projected on that screen, except his own distinct image. As he complains in the novel's opening page, when people look at him all they see are "my surroundings, themselves, or figment of their imagination – indeed everything and anything except me."[31] Invisibility is foremost an existential, before it is a social calamity.

Ellison's revolutionary response to the social disaster and moral disgrace of invisibility was to elaborate an aesthetics/politics of audibility. In his introduction to the novel, Ellison describes its origins in an earlier work whose narrative was "upstaged" by "a voice which spoke so knowingly of visibility" (IM, p.xi). The novel is Ellison's attempt to embody and record the testimony of this "taunting disembodied voice" and channel its uncanny power and authority. This explains how the protagonist-prophet who defines himself as the Invisible Man comes to know and realize himself as a Voice, a Voice, that whether speaking on the high or low frequencies, whether parroting racial bromides, ranting against social and economic discrimination, prophesying a new mode of racial and American identity, demonstrably possesses the power to penetrate the barriers of consciousness – the frontline of defense for every *pseudospecies*. Voice is not a property of Ellison's narrative, but its essence and objective. Ellison himself claims that it was not his invisibility, but his audibility that made his protagonist "without question a 'character,' and that in the dual meaning of the term" (IM, p.xix).

His being a character may be without question, but what duality he epitomizes is less so. The most immediate dual meaning that suggests itself is character as a novelistic personage and character in the American idiomatic sense of an eccentric. But the Invisible Man's dual character can support other dualities, some not as easily reconciled. The duality of his being both an individual character and a representative one, for example. The Invisible Man, like Ellison himself, is torn between his existential need to define himself in his own terms and his moral need to speak on behalf of his race, itself subdivided into a series of overlapping *pseudospecies* whose interests do not always coincide.

Ellison resolved this intrinsic and structural tension between Self-identity and Group-identity not through the stabilizing architectonics of myth, but in the more unstructured, fluid, improvisational magic of jazz. In a justly famous manifesto, Ellison celebrates jazz as the art of individual assertion within and against the group: "This is the art by which the artist – and by extension the self as a performer – may define his identity as individual, as a member of the collectivity and as a link in the chain of tradition."[32] Only an Identity that encompasses the individual, the group, and the traditions that link and unite them can be said to represent what Ellison, at the conclusion of *Invisible Man*, maintains is the true fate of character – "to become one, yet many" – a pronouncement he insists is not prophecy but description (IM, p.577).

The problem, then, for the hero or heroine of the "Identity" bildungsroman is to become not one, but, as Ellison says, "one, yet many." It is a problem confronted and provisionally resolved in a less improvised way by Saleem Sinai, the protagonist of Salman Rushdie in *Midnight's Children*. Born on the stroke of that midnight when India became an independent modern nation, Saleem, by virtue of this historical accident, is also ineluctably fated to become "one, yet many." For him, too, the problem of the novel is to find a form to represent his dual character. The problem baffles, but does not defeat him: "How, in what terms, may the career of a single individual be said to impinge on the fate of a nation? I must answer in adverts and hyphens: I was linked to history both literally and metaphorically, both actively and passively, in what our (admirably modern) scientists might term 'modes of connection' composed of 'dualistically-combined configurations' of the two pairs of opposed adverts given above. This is why hyphens are necessary; actively-literally, passively-metaphorically, actively-metaphorically and passively-literally, I was inextricably entwined within my world."[33] Hyphens are not only the necessary but also the preferable mode of connection between beleaguered Self and group identity. They typographically and semantically preserve the integrity of the antithetical self in all its various "dualistically-combined configurations." The hyphenated Identity is a way for the Self to define itself over and against the *pseudospecies*, which refuses to mingle and mix.

The need to preserve the rudiments of the Self in the fortress of (group) Identity is recast as a more militant tale in Maxine Hong Kingston's *A Woman Warrior*, a novel in which the act of self-expression is itself regarded as a kind of martial art. The forces and objects with which the Self is embattled are all those potential definers of identity: gender, sexuality, race, ethnicity, class, religion, nationality. How the Self might assert and triumph over these forces and what, indeed, such a victory might mean is what the writing of the novel is to determine. The narrator, the Chinese-American descendant of the No Name Woman who gives the novel its proud but generic title, fires the first salvo in the battle for self-determination. "Chinese Americans," she at once asks and challenges her own *pseudospecies*,

> when you try to understand what things in you are Chinese, how do you separate what is peculiar to childhood, to poverty, insanities, one family, your mother who marked your growing with stories, from what is Chinese? What is Chinese tradition and what are movies?[34]

The hyphen at once connects and separates group identity (in this instance Chinese) from the entire envelope of circumstances that define the Self – the peculiar childhood, material poverty, insanities, and rationalities, one's own family and the mother who bore and morally shaped you with her stories. It serves as a bridge between private self and collective identity, reality and the fictions generated out or in spite of it, but it is also a marker of ineluctable separateness, of ultimate unmergeability. It is this double function that recommends the hyphen to the novel of modern, multicultural life, a literary form dedicated to building bridges from one Self to another, but also to defending what is distinctive, singular, inassimilable. The hyphenated Identity is one way the modern novel represents character as one, yet many.

We began by attending to the egg hatching in the garden during that historic year during which human character changed. It has hatched by now, so let us now turn to the new life form it seems to have been incubating – a new species of character, as it turns out, that transcends the confines of group and hyphenated Identity. A new species deserves its own name, so I have christened it the Native Cosmopolitan.

Endnotes

1 Virginia Woolf, "Mr. Bennett and Mrs. Brown," *The Captain's Death Bed and Other Essays* (New York: Mariner, 1973), p.94. Woolf, of course, was being deliberately disingenuous in dismissing the significance of the date she did choose, knowing full well that 1910 was notable for the death of King Edward the VII, the monarch who embodied the material riches, the sensual pleasures, the insouciant and privileged manners of a social and economic order most lavishly and ironically commemorated in Maddox Ford's *The Good Soldier*; for Roger Fry's mounting the First of two Post-Impressionist Exhibits; for the founding of the International Psychoanalytic Association. None of these events were revolutionary in themselves, but combined with each other they contributed to and intensified the general modern feeling that nothing was or would ever again be as it was. The arts were particularly influential as catalysts of change, since they helped transform the ways human beings saw themselves. Human character changed because it was seen differently– through the more experimental and, according to Woolf, the more "spiritual" art of the Georgian modernists like James Joyce, D. H. Lawrence, T. S. Eliot, and Woolf herself;

through a new painterly demonstration of the powers of light to dissolve, even as it momentarily delineated, the shimmering outlines of stable-seeming forms of the Natural world; through the psychoanalytic discovery of the Unconscious and the instinctual basis of the mental life.

2 Virginia Woolf, *The Waves* (San Diego, New York: Harcourt, Brace Jovanovich, 1959), p. 289. Hereafter W.

3 Franco Moretti, *The Way of the World* (New York: Verso, 1987), p. 228.

4 Saul Bellow, "The Future of Fiction," reprinted in *Saul Bellow and his Critics*, ed. Irving Malin (New York: NYU Press, 1967), p. 211.

5 Lewis Thomas, *The Medusa and the Snail* (New York: Penguin, 1995), p. 2.

6 Ralph Waldo Emerson, "Self-Reliance," *Essays First and Second Series* (New York: Library of America, 1990), p. 306.

7 William James, *Principles of Psychology*, Vol. I (New York: Dover, 1950), p. 291.

8 James, 1950, p. 292.

9 Thomas Carlyle, *Sartor Resartus* (New York: Oxford University Press, 2008), p. 55.

10 Virginia Woolf, *Mrs Dalloway* (New York: Penguin, 1992), p. 9. Henceforth MD.

11 Virginia Woolf, *The Diary of Virginia Woolf*. Vol. 2 (London: Hogarth, 1975), p. 248.

12 James, 1950, p. 316.

13 James, 1950, p. 330.

14 Sigmund Freud, *The Standard Edition of the Complete Psychological Works*, Vol. XI (London: Hogarth, 1975), pp. 153–61.

15 Virginia Woolf, *Orlando* (New York: Harcourt, Inc., 2006), p. 237.

16 Beckett is quick to make and reinforce this point in remarking that Murphy's mind "excluded nothing that it did not itself contain."

17 Virginia Woolf, *The Diary of Virginia Woolf*, Vol. 5 (San Diego, New York and London: Harcourt Brace Jovanovich, 1984), p. 135.

18 James Joyce, *Ulysses* (New York: Vintage, 1986), p. 174. Hereafter U.

19 Kenneth Burke, *A Grammar of Motives* (Berkeley: University of California, 1969), p. 300.

20 Rudyard Kipling, *Kim* (New York: Penguin, 1987), p. 338.

21 E. M. Forster, *A Passage to India* (San Diego: Harcourt Brace, 1984), p. 37. Henceforth PI.

22 Kenneth Burke, *Language as Symbolic Action* (Berkeley: University of California Press, 1966), p. 238.

23 D. H. Lawrence, *Sons and Lovers* (New York: Modern Library, 1986), p. 6.

24 D. H. Lawrence, "Study of Thomas Hardy," *Phoenix* (New York; Viking, 1968), p. 432.
25 D. H. Lawrence, *The Letters of D. H. Lawrence*, Vol. 2 (Cambridge: Cambridge University Press, 2002), p. 183.
26 D. H. Lawrence, "Foreword," *Women in Love* (New York: Penguin, 2004), p. 484.
27 James Joyce, *A Portrait of the Artist as a Young Man* (New York: Penguin, 1993) p. 12.
28 Eric Erikson, *Identity, Youth and Crisis* (W. W. Norton: New York, 1968), p. 16.
29 Erikson, 1968, p. 41.
30 Erikson, 1968, p. 44.
31 Ralph Ellison, *Invisible Man* (New York: Vintage, 1980) p. 3. Hereafter IM.
32 Ralph Ellison, *Shadow and Act* (New York: Vintage, 1985), p. 235.
33 Salman Rushdie, *Midnight's Children* (New York: Penguin, 1991), pp. 272–3. Hereafter MC.
34 Maxine Hong Kingston, *The Woman Warrior: Memoirs of a Girlhood Among Ghosts* (New York: Vintage, 1989), p. 5.

III

Compounds

5

Native Cosmopolitans

"How does newness come into the world?" is a question for the end of epochs – and books, like this one, preoccupied with the changing fortunes of *novelistic* character. This particular version of the question is posed at the beginning of Salman Rushdie's *The Satanic Verses*, where it alerts us that the world we have known, often (if we are lucky) have loved, and frequently despaired of, is approaching exhaustion and that now is the time to be wondering where and how to introduce something new and vital into its depleted midst.

Rushdie begins his search for an answer where a novelist would instinctively look – in an image of human creatures undergoing, in this instance suffering, metamorphosis: two distinct figures (both actors, hence already accomplished in, and presumably devoted to, the arts of self-transformation) plummeting from the sky after the plane in which they were traveling explodes, instantly transformed into a "seedpod giving up its spores, an egg yielding its mystery."[1] As they plunge toward the earth, they apparently still have enough of their wits about them to wonder:

Who am I?
who else is there?

Given that physical extinction appears to be just seconds away, questions about who we are and if we are accompanied are almost comically irrelevant. The absurdity of asking them in such dire circumstances is itself evidence of how seriously Rushdie considers them to be.

From such slender, but undeniably dramatic evidence, we might deduce two axiomatic principles concerning the genesis and enduring preoccupations of the novel as a distinct cultural form. First axiom: The novel, even if it forswears the verbal and scenic wonders, calculated outrages, and preposterous scenarios of Rushdiean fantasy, is a seedpod bursting with germinating life. Second axiom: The novel, whatever its chosen environment, narrative idiom, and plot trajectory, is generically disposed to ask two primary questions about the *character* of human life. The first we might call the Crusoe question, the question of the solitary human being confronted with the physical and moral reality of his unique existence; the second is also a Crusoe question and follows upon the first – who else is there taking up space and moral room beside and among me?

Yet while there may be nothing particularly new in the questions even the most up-to-date fiction asks of its characters, there seems to be less and less (islanded, private) space in which to ask them. Character wants room, as Emerson advised (and warned) us, but at the approach and dawn of the millennium, when more and more life is lived in overcrowded, over-scrutinized spaces, open expanses for the development, exploration, reinvention, or consolidation of character are rapidly contracting; those that remain are not easily accessible or hardly habitable—witness the bleak post-apocalyptic landscapes of Cormac McCarthy's *The Road*.

In such conditions, the questions facing characters free-falling into modernity are, as Rushdie's desperate fiction suggests, perhaps best, even if hurriedly, asked, in mid-air, "the most insecure and transitory of zones, illusory, discontinuous metamorphic" (S, p.5). However insecure, not to mention inhospitable the upper atmosphere may be for human life, there is nonetheless abundant room, if little time, for a character to summon and exert its inward force. Rushdie, driven by temperament and the barbarisms of modern history into brash, desperate, and absurdist comedy, seems to relish the notion that once "you throw everything up in the air anything becomes possible." We might balk at the untested confidence conveyed by that "anything," yet be perfectly willing to suspend our disbelief long enough to entertain the narrator's assertion that "way up there, … changes took place in delirious actors that would have gladdened the heart of old Mr Larmarck: under extreme environmental pressure, characteristics were acquired" (S, p.5).

These changes should also gladden the devoted readers of novels, connoisseurs of character. They augur a future in which the novel will continue to be a seedpod bursting with new life forms. They also confirm the novel's predisposition to conceive of character and account for its development in Lamarckian terms. The hypothesis that traits can be acquired – and transmitted to succeeding generations – has been the working, if unstated assumption of the novel even before Lamarck formulated it. The starved soul of Don Quijano, subsisting on a meager diet of lentils and the parched landscapes of La Mancha that feed his madness, imaginatively reacts and rebels against the pressures of his impoverished life by conceiving a nobler and richer version of himself. To this ideal self he gives the name Don Quixote, a Lamarckian wonder who will become the patriarch of a novelistic line of spiritual adventurers undeterred by the crude evidence of empirical reality in their quest for moral beauty. A mad project, of course, and therein lies one of the key insights of the novel in its representations of human possibility. The novel has always been more skeptical than hopeful that adaptability ensures the survival of the morally sensitive, as it seems to do for the physically fittest, of our kind. This skepticism becomes a Darwinian commonplace in the mid-Victorian novel, as instanced in the poignant figure of Philip Wakem, whose fine emotional nature is burdened by a "puny, miserable body." Wakem's disfigurement will become more widespread among the emotionally bereft, disabled heroes of early twentieth-century fiction. Prominent among the ranks of such sympathetic, but physically disadvantaged characters are Rickie Elliot in E. M. Forster's *The Longest Journey*, Philip Carey in

Somerset Maugham's underrated *Of Human Bondage*, James Flory, the protagonist of George Orwell's *Burmese Days*, whose face is disfigured by a dark, blue birthmark; or, most unnervingly, the injury suffered by Jake Barnes, the "hero"-narrator of Hemingway's *The Sun Also Rises*, whose notorious "war wound" confirms as much as it accounts for and symbolizes the moral impotence of the Lost Generation.

Nor are female characters exempt from such genetic misfortunes. There is, most notably, the pathetic-bathetic figure of Gerty McDowell, the modern, proletarian Nausica and "jilted beauty" of Joyce's *Ulysses*, whose lovely, virginal form is marred by the limp she reveals as she takes leave of the beach, the man, and the novel she had entertained with her seductive seaside poses; or, the more extravagantly imagined Prudence Sarn, the heroine of Mary Webb's lavish tribute to Hardy's dark pastorals, *Precious Bane*, who is born with a harelip. (In the astonishing last line of the novel, Webb, who herself suffered from a facial disfigurement caused by Graves disease, dares the supreme romantic gesture in modern fiction without a glint of irony.)

Such disfiguring and crippling afflictions will metastasize into the systemic disintegration that Beckett's Molloy, Moran, Malone, and – deteriorating so exquisitely that he no longer requires a personal name – the Unnamable endure with grim determination (and, increasingly, with obvious relief) before they mutate once more into the indigenous postwar, postcolonial psychological disorders of V. S. Naipaul's "mimic men", the flat affect and pathological reserve of Ishiguro's traumatized narrators, and the chronic melancholia of W. G. Sebald's distressed wanderers, who, despairing of history, seek shelter, if not illumination, in twilight realms of steadily declining light.

A dispiriting survey, yet a morally and emotionally compelling one. It suggests that the environmental pressures to which self-consciously modern or helplessly contemporary characters are subject are more extreme, psychologically confusing, and potentially more spirit-deforming than those to which Tom Jones, Emma Woodhouse, Pip, Madame Bovary, Jude (the Obscure) Fawley, and even weak-eyed, but morally robust Stephen Dedalus, in flight from the entangling nets of family, nation, and religion, were exposed.

It is not just that the social field in which novelistic characters are now being born is populated with more and different types of people living according to diverse, sometimes competing customs, religious beliefs, social rites, and ways of thinking. It is that the world into which we are born, make our home, and find our way, has become at once less awesome and more strange. It is less awesome because the world is traversable as never before: economic migrants, political refugees, voluntary exiles, not to mention business and leisure travelers, voyage further and in less time than Don Quixote ever dreamed or Conrad's seafarers dared hope. Transcontinental flight, as Rushdie's opening signals and as the transnational fiction of V. S. Naipaul, Nadine Gordimer, J. M. Coetzee, Anita and Kiran Desai, Zadie Smith, Jhumpa Lahirri, and Edwige Danticat routinely dramatize, is now within reach of the poorest and lowliest of the world's migratory populations.

But the world has also become a stranger, less familiar place as local communities are amalgamated into larger social and economic regimes: global trademarks (Coke, Nike, Apple, Sony) now make one place seem eerily like another, while the indigenous landmarks that served to guide us through experience – local traditions, a shared and heritable Past – seem to be stationed farther and farther apart. Immigrant attempts to replicate their home culture in foreign lands – the countless Little Italys, Chinatowns, Jewish quarters, the barrios, and Middle or Near or Far Eastern enclaves that settle in and transform whole neighborhoods – are meeting with more limited and transient success. The cosmopolitan metropolis is desegregating itself and recombining its ethnic populations in surprising new ways. Neighborhoods quickly change their character, some actually collapsing into each other, juxtaposing and scrambling cultural identities in a crazy quilt of internationalist enterprise. How crazy, at times demented, the pattern can be inspires some of the most concentrated, precise notations of Richard Price's richly idiomatic, naturalist detective procedural, *Lush Life*. In the novel's near-literal tour de force opening, Price describes the night rounds of the officers of the smartly named Quality of Life Task Force as they thread through a "honeycomb of narrow streets," negotiating the seemingly "endless tight right turns" of the Lower East Side of Manhattan – symbol and mecca of generations of immigrants seeking refuge, asylum, and economic opportunity in the New World. These are the way stations of the Quality of Life nightly Pilgrimage:

> falafel joint, jazz joint, gyro joint, corner. Schoolyard, crêperie, realtor, corner. Tenement, tenement, tenement museum, corner. Pink Pony. Blind Tiger, muffin boutique, corner. Sex shop, tea shop, synagogue, corner. Boulangerie, bar, hat boutique, corner. Iglesia, gelateria, matzo shop, corner. Bollywood, Buddha, botanica, corner. Leather outlet, leather outlet, leather outlet, corner. Bar, school, bar, school, People's park, corner. Tyson mural, Celia Cruz mural, Lady Di mural, corner. Bling shop, barbershop, car service, corner.[2]

Whatever new life emerges in novels written about or in response to these rapidly mutating, polyglot, multicultural environments may no longer hope to possess, much less secure a cultural heritage that is discrete and relatively intact. In the modern metropolis, figures as distant from each other in background, talent, and cultural importance as a bruising heavy-weight fighter, a Cuban salsa singer who spent most of her life in exile, and a bona fide Princess in a fractured contemporary fairy tale share the same commemorative space.

It is in such unfamiliar, ever mutating, and often unwelcoming environments that transplanted, migrant, and Quixotic characters of the postwar, postcolonial world find themselves, as Rushdie reports, surrounded by "the debris of the soul, broken memories, sloughed-off selves, severed mother-tongues, violated privacies, untranslatable jokes, extinguished futures, lost loves, the forgotten meaning of hollow, booming words, *land, belonging, home*" (S, p.4). This list is stunning in the deprivations and devastation it records – the loss of memory, love, language; the forksaken privacies, abandoned hilarities, and extinguished futures. Strikingly, Rushdie's lamentation seems to crest and then expend itself in recounting the loss, to both writer and man, of those primal words – land, belonging, home. He seems to take a kind of savage comfort in recognizing that these talismanic words, over which societies have and still do fight with uncommon ferocity, have been hollowed out of the rich, soul-sustaining meaning they once possessed.

Rushdie has made no mystery of why he feels at once aggrieved, bewildered, but also energized as he enters a literary domain littered with cultural debris and occupied by disoriented, often disintegrating personalities. In his nonfictional work he has eloquently envisioned the more humane and imaginatively congenial prospect – for the writer at least – of imaginary, as opposed to actual, historic homelands. The cinematic Land of Oz, a dream-realm that Rushdie has written suspiciously as well as delightedly about, is one paradigm for the imaginary homeland – a nowhere that is the Elsewhere to which the Uprooted long to escape.[3] Of course Rushdie knows all too well that both Oz and Dorothy's home have no links to known places outside of a Kansas fabricated on a studio backlot. His own fictions are occasioned by, and fashioned out of the nightmares of history from which Stephen Dedalus hoped, but failed to awake. *Midnight's Children*, Rushdie's inaugural work, established a novelistic template for a new kind of historical fiction that succeeding novels will elaborate with varying degrees of ingenuity: History as the Demon Mother of violently proliferating, self-ravaging forms. The novel is a chronicle of the fortune of her blighted offspring: Saleem Sinai, the child of midnight who narrates the novel, his evil twin and more sympathetic siblings, all possessed of magic and metamorphic powers; a newborn nation whose metamir Saleem is ordained, indeed conscripted, to become.

Metamir, not mirror image. A subtle but necessary distinction to keep in mind if we are to understand the personal predicament and the cultural role of the Rushdiean creative character, itself a prototype of the "new" artistic character of the novel at the end of one century and the beginning of another. The term has undergone its own subtle transmutations from its first coinage in Primo Levi's 1985 short story, "The Mirror Maker," to its memorable evocation in Nadine Gordimer's *Writing and Being*, where it takes on a meaning that is particularly relevant to Saleem's unwonted – and unwanted – destiny. In the course of her personal reflections on the relation between imaginary characters and their real-life (often quite ordinary) counterparts, Gordimer suddenly introduces the more abstruse figure of Levi's metamir, that "metaphysical mirror" that "does not obey the law of optics but reproduces your image as it is seen by the person who stands before you."[4] So defined, the metamir serves Gordimer to illustrate the unique imaginative power of the writer before the realities she beholds. The writer is the metamir who reflects, Gordimer insists, "a series of intimations ...not present to the ordinary mirror of the world."[5]

The Rushdiean metamir is at once more grandiose and more subservient than the reflective figure Gordimer describes. History, like the monster mother she generally proves herself to be, claims Saleem, midnight's child and Rushdie's narrator/protagonist/alter-ego, as her own and enlists him to serve her own transhuman ends. As narrator/metamir Saleem is made to stand not just *before* but *for* the history of his nation, whose birth-pangs coincided with his own fateful entry into the world – midnight, 1947 (the year of Rushdie's own birth). Although he will find himself, like so many of Rushdie's narrators, writing in some undisclosed place or prison far removed from the streets, markets, courts, parliaments, and royal precincts of power where History is daily enacted, Saleem begins the world in perfect synchrony with History as it is embodied in the Epochal Moment. The uncanny timing of his birth threatens to overshadow any distinct character he might acquire. Midway through the novel, Saleem somewhat dispiritedly recounts that when the Indian Prime Minister had written him with assurances that "Your life will be, in a sense, the mirror of our own," he felt obliged "scientifically to ask the question: In what sense?" (MC, p.285). More than uncertainty or confusion prompt Saleem's question about the nature and extent of his own historical representativeness. The knowledge – or the repeated insistence of others – that he is at the center of things brings Saleem no pleasure, no exhibitionist rush; it certainly does not lead to a serene understanding and acceptance of his place in the world. Quite the contrary. Nothing could disconcert and frighten him more than being at the center of things that he neither fully understands nor even partially controls.

This burden of being representative of a people, a country, and a time because History and not your own Willful or Exemplary Character makes you so, marks a new Lamarckian development in the evolution of novelistic character. There is little to celebrate in this development, as Rushdie's characters can tell you. They are born or aspire to a centrality that confers no real power and brings little, if any personal satisfaction. Their subservience to their assigned historical role marks a stunning departure from the largeness of spirit and moral command that characterized the "real historical personalities" who dominated the novels of Sir Walter Scott. These grand beings are the exemplary heroes of Georg Lukács's *The Historical Novel*. Lukács commends Scott's "historical faithfulness" in portraying the greatness of the hero – or heroine! – whose personality is "representative of an important and significant movement embracing large sections of the people." Less an active figure than a reflective metamir of his age, Saleem can still boast special powers, but not the greatness that distinguished the Scott hero, who, in Lukács's estimation, is "great because his personal passion and personal aim coincide with this great historical movement, because he concentrates within himself its positive and negative sides, because he gives to these popular strivings their clearest expression, because he is their standard-bearer in good and in evil."[6]

Saleem may not be a morally forceful standard-bearer, but he proves marvelously constituted to channel the popular strivings of his own historical moment. Despite the fact that neither his personal passion nor personal aim coincide with the larger currents of his historical moment, his fantastic powers make him a Public Transmitter for the *vox populi*, a phrase he literally comes to embody. Even though Saleem, as both a narrator and self-chronicler, inherits and at various instances makes use of all the novelistic tools – free indirect discourse, tracking the random (Lockean) association of ideas, stream of consciousness – developed to excavate the life of the mind, he finds his narrative consciousness increasingly invaded by incoming signals, many of them sent in distress. Because of their number, volume, and variety, Saleem justifiably thinks of his mind as the central receiving station for an unauthorized, unlicensed telecommunications marvel – All-India Radio – through which reverberate "the inner monologues of all the so-called millions, of masses and classes alike" (MC, p.200). Beneath the "polyglot frenzy" of voices jostling for space within his head – voices babbling "in everything from Malayaam to Naga dialects, from the purity of Lucknow Urdu to the Southern slurring of Tamil," Saleem eventually begins to discriminate "universally intelligible thought-forms which far transcend words … precious signals, utterly different from everything else, most of them faint and distant, like far off drums whose insistent pulsing eventually broke through the fish-market cacophony of my voices." These "secret nocturnal calls, like calling out to like," are found to be signaling "nothing more than their existence, transmitting simply 'I.' From far to the North, 'I.' And the South East West 'I.' 'I.' And 'I' "(MC, p.200).

These nocturnal transmissions of like calling out to like should not be dismissed as the narcissistic bleatings of bereft or bored souls yearning for attention or simply the company of their kind. I take these transmissions to be distress signals of struggling, threatened character, like those equally succinct, desperate, often banal messages circulated through the Tristero, the mysterious communication system in Thomas Pynchon's *The Crying of Lot 49*, in which like calls out to like in the shared language of the alienated and dispossessed. Coming from the four geographical coordinates, these "I"s may eventually congregate to form a new novelistic universe in which the "utterly different" human being might successfully resist total assimilation into the ethnic, racial or national group, defy the standardizations of the market and workplace, and outrun or outwit the sweeping, collectivizing movements of history.

But not here, not now. Pynchon's novel, set in the pre-apocalyptic terrain of 1960s' America, ends on the brink of revelation, awaiting the long-hoped for arrival of "that magical Other" who might be either the Angel of Death or the Prophet come to restore the legacy of America[7] where the chances for diversity were once so good. Rushdie is a less daring fantasist than Pynchon, who is not reluctant, as

Rushdie is, to admit genuine Mystery into his novels. For all the supernaturalism that lifts his novels from the flatlands of naturalistic chronicle, Rushdie ultimately capitulates to the Demon Mother of History, who prevents him from seeking – from stalking! – the magical or transcendent Other whose luminous presence would abolish the night. Madmen dominate Rushdie's fiction, but even in *The Moor's Last Sigh*, his tribute to Cervantes' lunatic Original, none of his protagonists possess Don Quixote's imaginative valor nor his dedication to moral beauty. Unlike Cervantes' mad knight, they still see the world in the light of common day and through the shadows of History. Rushdie can only hope to weaken, since he cannot completely relax, the stranglehold of history by endowing his characters, as he does Saleem, with "a fallible memory compounded by quirks of character and of circumstance."[8] Thus, for example, in Saleem's account of events, Mahatma Gandhi will be assassinated on the wrong date. Many novelists, Dickens most pre-eminently, have appreciated how quirks of character represent unconscious protests against the soul-distortions of oppressive social conventions and poor spiritual as well as economic environments. But rarely are such quirky characters called upon to resist the monolithic Force of History.

Rushdie, a fantasist hyper-conscious of his obligations to history and to truth, few, if any of them happily accepted, admits that not only the quirks of his narrators, but that of his own character as a writer are intensified by the circumstances of his own distance from India. These circumstances oblige him "to deal in broken mirrors, some of whose fragments have been irretrievably lost." Nonetheless, Rushdie immediately goes on to insist that "the broken mirror may actually be as valuable as the one which is supposedly unflawed." We could easily, perhaps too easily, read Rushdie's praise of brokenness as an imaginative attempt to console himself for the loss of a heritage that has been shattered or dispersed beyond restoration. But the compensations he discovers (or invents) are real, as real as his imagination can make them. Rushdie shows us how simple as well as real these compensations are when he relates how an old song came back to and remained with him during the writing of *Midnight's Children*, a song he offers up as Saleem's theme song. Here is the song:

> Mera Joota hai Japani
> Yé patloon Inglistani
> Sar pé la topi Rusi
> Phir bhi dil hai Hindustani
> O, my shoes are Japanese
> These trousers English, if you please
> On my head, red Russian hat
> My heart is Indian for all that.[9]

What is fetching, and in fact endearing about this folk song is the ebullient figure of its cheerful singer, who, clothed in the fashions of other cultures, has not lost his sense and his love of himself – his heart remains "Indian for all that." Without a name, sporting only an attitude, this singer is, in V. S. Naipaul's morally rich phrase, self-cherishing.

How self-cherishing is made clear by comparing this particoloured singer festooned in multinational garments to his more manic and overly romantic kin – the young Russian adventurer who is "Kurtz's last disciple" in Conrad's *The Heart of Darkness*. Both in the genial folk song and in Marlow's grimly humorous description of the harlequin figure whose plain brown Holland clothes are "covered with patches all over, with bright patches, blue, red, and yellow," the human figure seems to dissolve into a kind of multicultural mirage. Such motley figures appear bizarre even to an eye as accustomed to exotic costumes and foreign manners as Marlow's, who initially finds the young Russian not just baffling, but uninterpretable: "He was an insoluble problem," Marlow affirms. "It was inconceivable how he had existed, how he had succeeded in getting so far, how he managed to remain – why he did not instantly disappear."[10]

But of course he doesn't disappear. Rather, he obligingly leads Marlow deeper into the heart of darkness, where Kurtz awaits them both. Kurtz, that much condemned and over-read but still mysterious man: he has been reviled as the corrupt incarnation of imperious Enlightenment thought and the Empire created, administered, and justified by its principles. But I see him as something more prescient and just as scary: the grim specter of the modern cosmopolitan gone native. Viewed in Lamarckian terms, he represents an evolutionary misfire, the traits he acquired as an agent – the supreme agent – of international mercantile capitalism rendering him unfit to exist as anything other than a human incarnation of "the horror, the horror." Kurtz, whose name, meaning short, was, as Marlow remarks, as deceptive as much else about the man, casts a long shadow on the cosmopolitan and native ordeals to come. His moral collapse presages horrible Lamarckian adaptations to the incessant infiltration of foreign power and influences, both beneficent and malign, into native spheres, incursions that affect not just local economies, but cultural manners, social reflexes, fashions, physical mannerisms, language, ways of living – and dying.

Native Cosmopolitans

Such motley characters, in their selective relation or dark enthrallment to the idols of international commerce, are forerunners and prototypes of an emerging individuality that the novelist-as-metamir puts before us. In their most attractive guise, they are harbingers of a new breed of character that we might call Native Cosmopolitans. These strange, often shy and as yet somewhat inchoate beings are what Kurtz may have initially aspired, but horrendously failed, to become. In their less monstrous but still eccentric incarnations, they represent a new kind of character, one formed in the enduring *ethos* of local traditions and habits but marked (stunned, traumatized, exhilarated) by the consciousness that one is more connected to, yet less at home in the larger human world. Saleem, himself a child of midnight straddling the imperial past and the nationalist/cosmopolitan future, offers us a mythical way of understanding this new novelistic character when he evokes the spirit of the Gander, "the mythical bird, the hamsa or parahamsa, symbol of the ability to live in two worlds, the physical and the spiritual, the world of land-and-water and the world of air, of flight" (MC, p.255). Native Cosmopolitans are neither mythical nor symbolic creatures; yet they, too, possess or hope to develop the ability to live in two worlds: the native and the global, the homeland (real or imaginary) and the place where they happen, through accident or by design, to abide. Note: though they can live in two worlds, they cannot do so at once.

More but also less than a paradox is intended in designating these new novelistic subjects as Native Cosmopolitans, terms usually opposed to each other and here unexpectedly conjoined. In such close proximity, we can appreciate how fluid their meanings have become in modern usages. The more unstable, historically vexed, and compromised term is the word native, as commonly referring to someone born in a particular place or community. This usage is not as simple or innocent as it might initially appear. Being born in a particular place is no longer (if it ever was) enough to ensure that the native *feels* like a native, that is, feels at home even and especially after time spent in other places, cities, countries. This unhappy possibility lurks within the title of Thomas Hardy's *The Return of the Native* as an irony ready to assert and fulfill itself. As it does with a vengeance in making an example of the luckless Clym Yeobright, a native Oedipus who returns to his maternal home after experiencing and tiring of the cosmopolitan life of Paris, only to meet and marry that dark enchantress, Eustacia Vye, the native beauty who yearns for Paris as for a transfiguration. The community has no real place for them and they are of little moral use to each other in their striving for self-realization. Is it any wonder that one must die and the other end his days a sightless preacher? Lawrence objected, rightly in my view, to "the subtle equivocation" in Clym's taking on the "commission for society to enlighten the souls of others," rather than, to use Lawrence's matchless and quite precise idiom, "to struggle at the quick to bring himself into being." His refusal to "undertake his own soul," leads to a new kind of tragic outcome, the failure to become what Lawrence calls "an integral man."[11] Lawrence may be the last novelist to believe that it is possible to attain an integral character – that is, a character that is whole unto itself, untouched, as its root meaning indicates, by the impositions of social convention (hence Lawrence's importance in the history of novelistic character).

Hardy's tragic natives – Clym, Eustacia, Tess of the d'Urbervilles, Jude the Obscure – enact their fate against a background that gives their death a pathos, even a majesty, denied their forlorn descendents. So much is evident in their doomed modern American counterparts, the doubly dispossessed native sons of American cities. Their plight is searingly recorded in Richard Wright's novel-as-indictment, *Native Son*. The title bristles with irony, reproach, lamentation. Wright's screed against the endemic and toxic racism that poisons American life is amplified by the sardonic emphasis he gives the word native in his title. Its prominence recalls, retains, and reinforces the pernicious rather than chauvinistic meaning of the word "native" that dates to medieval times, in which the native referred to a person born in bondage, a word cognate with naïf in its original but now obsolete sense of someone born in serfdom. Imperial and colonial orders inherited and expanded on this dehumanizing legacy in speaking of the native as a lesser order of humankind. To the moral iniquity of these associations, the practices and mores of international capitalism have added another – the commodification of the native as both a consumer and a quaint or picturesque, thus highly marketable, tourist attraction rather than a vital person and forceful presence with living roots in the local community.

Both views of the native are summoned in the "return of the native" that opens *A Way in the World*, one of Naipaul's many fictional accounts of a return to his native Trinidad.

> I left home more than forty years ago. I was eighteen. When I went back, after six years – and slowly: a two-week journey by steamer – everything was strange and not strange: the suddenness of night, the very big leaves of some trees, the shrunken streets, the corrugated-iron roofs. You could walk down a street and hear the American advertising jingles coming out of the Rediffusion sets in all the little open houses. Six years before I had known the jingles

> the Rediffusion sets played; but these jingles were all new to me and were like somebody else's folksong now.[12]

A folksong, Rushdie claimed, had transported and repatriated him to his imaginary homeland. Naipaul's narrator re-enters a world in which advertising jingles for American products sound like new folksongs foreign to his ears. The moment is paradigmatic, perhaps falsely so, since it is not immediately clear why American jingles would sound so strangely in the narrator's ears. He has not been marooned, like Crusoe, on an island, but returned from metropolitan London where such jingles could not have been all that uncommon.

Such returns of the native, in their very ambiguity, are exemplary of the uncertain and confused status of the native as an integral character. They alert us to the ways in which the word native, used as a *noun,* is too burdened by history and its pitiless ironies to support by itself the complicated, often ethnically various, and culturally mixed nature of "local" characters. The word native is more trustworthy when used as an adjective, a marker of origin, than as a noun denoting a kind of *being* innate to a certain region or culture.

Cosmopolitan, on the other hand, is a word of sturdier and less morally compromised provenance, encompassing as it does both the culture and the personal orientation of a certain kind of human being who identifies with something beyond the local or indigenous population into which he or she happened to be born. I prefer the term cosmopolitan to words like global or international to describe the Larmarckian environment to which novelistic characters (and indeed actual persons) must adapt. The word global unnecessarily restricts us to earthly dimensions, when, as we shall see, it is to questions of the spirit that native cosmopolitanism responds. The word international is also limited, suggesting as it does a world of geopolitical alliances and rivalries. Cosmopolitan subsumes both the global and international without being limited or exhausted by their particular circle of reference. Moreover, as Anthony Appiah notes, it brings important associations of its own. The term was coined by the Cynic philosophers of the first century BC, to promote the idea of the individual whose primary affiliation and loyalty was as a "citizen of the cosmos." Cosmopolitanism reflected, Appiah goes on to remark, "the general Cynic skepticism toward custom and tradition. A citizen – a *polites* – belonged to a particular polis, and a city to which he or she owed loyalty. The cosmos referred to the world, not in the sense of the earth, but in the sense of the universe. Talk of cosmopolitanism originally signaled, then, a rejection of the conventional view that every civilized person belonged to a community among communities."[13]

This rejection of local traditions and affiliations was not total however. In issuing her clarion call for a cosmopolitan ethics and educational regime, Martha Nussbaum reminds us that the Stoics stressed "that to be a citizen of the world one does not need to give up local identifications, which can be a source of great richness in life."[14] On the contrary. As Nussbaum points out, the Stoics advised that we think of the Self in its relation to its immediate and extended environment as a series of eccentric circles. "The first one," explains Nussbaum

> encircles the self, the next takes in the immediate family, then follows the extended family; then, in order, neighbors or local groups, fellow city-dwellers, and fellow country-men – and we can easily add to this list groupings based on ethnic, linguistic, historical, professional, gender, or sexual identities. Outside all these circles is the largest one, humanity as a whole. Our task as a citizen of the world will be to "draw the circles somehow toward the center" (Stoic philosopher Hierocles, 1st–2nd CE), making all human beings more like our fellow city-dwellers and so on.[15]

So described, cosmopolitanism envisions the moral universe as a Ptolemaic one, with the self as a stationary or rooted point around which various circles of life and community revolve. This being so, we may, like Rushdie, scientifically object that the geopolitical universe is Copernican, thus making it somewhat difficult to follow the Stoic injunction to "draw the circles somehow toward the center," no matter how deft and sure our moral compass proves to be.

The Self may well find itself thinning out, becoming increasingly attenuated as it moves from its rooted core outward toward larger circles of association until it becomes somewhat featureless, almost transparent, once it takes its place within the circle of "humanity as a whole." Those securely and gladly situated within that larger circle of humanity may very well think of themselves as cosmopolitan natives whose attachments to various groups are consolidated in an all-embracing, warm circle of life. Who knows but that they may rightfully dream of taking up semi-permanent residence in some Upton Inn of the future, in which wayfarers of all classes and sects could commingle with robustly comical results.

But in our own tragico-farcical time – the time that gallops in Rushdie's manic fiction, provides the counterpoint for the absurdist comedy of Naipaul's postcolonial narratives, propels Phillip Roth's ranting chronicles of postwar American life – no such happy coincidence of center and periphery, self and larger humanity are to be observed, much less anticipated. For now, we are talking about characters for whom the center either does not hold or can no longer accommodate them. They are unsettled – yes, restless! – natives at home everywhere and nowhere. Such beings are not likely to envision their world as a series of concentric circles with ever expanding peripheries. Rather they, or at least the novel in which their predicament and opportunities are dramatized, are more likely to orient themselves by asking the very elementary sort of questions with which Rushdie's novel and our investigation into character begins: Who am I? Who else is there? Even if these questions can be satisfactorily answered, a third perplexity troubles their dawning moral awareness: to whom or to what, other than myself, do I owe allegiance as a human being?

This third question plaguing the congenitally cosmopolitan character, a question about its fundamental loyalties to people other than itself, shadows any hope we might entertain that cosmopolitanism would allow us to us fashion a universal and morally fortified Identity as a citizen of the world. Appiah is very sensitive to the potential for emotional hauteur among those self-proclaimed cosmopolitans whose sympathies are righteously engaged only with those who live

Elsewhere and Otherwise than themselves. But he is also dismayed by the restricted sympathies of the ardent nationalist. In extreme cases, he notes, there is "the nationalist who abandons all foreigners and the hard-core cosmopolitan who regards her friends and fellow citizens with icy impartiality. The position worth defending might be called (in both senses) partial cosmopolitanism."[16]

Such partiality offers us a reasoned and reasonable position, and is commendable, indeed endorsable and embraceable as such. But it represents a philosopher's, not a novelist's solution. A novelist, that is, might be more partial to the nativist than to the cosmopolitan character if for no other reason than the native is rooted in the daily routines, customs, and traditions that give a culture and its people their distinctive, continuous, if ever changing life. This is the great and insistent theme of Naipaul's writings, which chronicle – and lament – the erosion of naïve traditions, with their soul-sustaining, soul-enriching "own language, … families, clans, *ethnies*, religious practices, their own totems and household gods, their own instinctive reverences" (AWW, p. 138). Following Naipaul, we might indeed characterize the Native-Cosmopolitan novel, which finds its subject and moral compass in the ethos of home and national traditions, as *the* book of instinctive reverences for the language, family traditions, and household gods, the sacred and profane rituals that give texture and meaning to the everyday life of its characters.

Naipaul's respect for nativist sentiments and rituals was shared, indeed anticipated by George Eliot, another novelist concerned with the moral sentiments and instinctive reverences inculcated by familial and social traditions. Eliot, who figures importantly in Appiah's own arguments for a partial cosmopolitanism, understood and to a certain extent shared the Cynical skepticism toward tradition and custom, especially when it manifested itself in parochial, xenophobic, and, especially, anti-Semitic feeling. But this never led her to adopt, much less endorse, the perspective of the citizen of the world. In her last and least guarded work, *The Impressions of Theophrastus Such*, in which she develops an extended analogy between the Jewish diaspora and English natives living abroad, Eliot embraced a warmer partiality for nativist sentiments than Appiah perhaps would recommend. She criticized "the affectation of undervaluing everything native, and being too fine for one's own country." Eliot herself betrayed no such affectation. For her the native had a unique value: it promoted greatness as well as ease of character. She believed that for an individual to be "harmoniously great," he or she "must belong to a nation of this order, if not in actual existence, yet existing in the past, in memory, as a departed, invisible, beloved ideal, once a reality, and perhaps to be restored. A common humanity is not yet enough to feed the rich blood of various activity which makes a complete man." The time, she wrote in 1888, "has not come for cosmopolitanism to be highly virtuous, any more than for communism to suffice for social energy." Today's fervent cosmopolitans might well counter that the time has finally arrived. We shall see.

Far more than the passage of time and the technological changes, especially in telecommunications, that have transformed the world into a global village are needed for the cosmopolitan character to become a "complete" man – or woman. Eliot's moral reservations about cosmopolitan virtue derive from her belief that "[a]ffection, intelligence, duty, radiate from a centre." Eliot contends that

> countrymen who take to living abroad without purpose or function to keep up their sense of fellowship in the affairs of their own land, are rarely good specimens of moral healthiness; still, the consciousness of having a native country, the birthplace of common memories and habits of mind, existing like a parental hearth quitted but beloved; the dignity of being included in a people which has a part in the comity of nations and the growing federation of the world; that sense of special belonging which is the root of human virtues, both public and private – all these spiritual links may preserve migratory Englishmen from the worst consequences of their voluntary dispersion.[17]

Although Eliot's reflections show a marked affinity with Stoic notions of the moral benefits accruing to taking one's "part in the comity of nations and the growing federation of the world," she did not project a time or a world order when cosmopolitanism would actively minister to, rather than compromise the moral healthiness of the migratory native. This should not concern us unduly, since the value of her analysis is not prophetic, but moral and structural. Without resorting to mythical thinking, she was contemplating the historical and environmental conditions in which it might be possible to inhabit, like the hamsa bird, two worlds without losing one's foothold in the homeland or one's bearings in the larger federation of the world. The moral possibility of a Native Cosmopolitan was already in her sights.

Stereotypes and Mimic Men

Such a possibility was not likely to be realized, however, in Middlemarchian communities visited, but largely bypassed by modernity and its burgeoning economic and social multiculturalism. The modern metropolis, which attracts foreigners to its midst, offered a more promising ground for seeding new strains of character. The initial results are not heartening. They point to the difficulty of becoming a fully fledged character in a metropolitan environment in which demographic labels abound and a single trait stands for entire personalities. Hence the air of depression that hangs about and weighs down this chapter in the history of novelistic character, which began with so much hope for a new life-form, what I have called the Native Cosmopolitan, to usher the way into a brave new world of transculturalism. The Larmarckian adaptations chronicled in fiction after fiction in the postwar, postcolonial world are hardly specimens of moral healthiness. Naipaul, in a pitiless and discouraging phrase, has called them mimic men, displaced or voluntarily relocated natives who are dispirited, disoriented, at a loss in answering for themselves or for anyone else they happen to live among.

Their experience is epitomized in the unhappy aphorism that summarizes the moral knowledge acquired by the aspiring colonial politician/writer/narrator of Naipaul's *Mimic Men* from his life in London after the war: "Once a man is stripped of his dignities he is required, not to die or to run away, but to find his level."[18] In fulfillment of this degrading requirement, he initially rooms in a "boardinghouse which between attic and basement, pleasure and its penalty, we boarders lived, narrowly."[18] Character, which needs room and craves expansion, finds itself miserably confined. Narrowness of room, contraction of experience: these are the environmental conditions in which the mimic men, in flight from their native culture, emerge as the sorriest sub-species of Native Cosmopolitans. The narrator, conscious of having known "grandeur beyond the football-pool dreams" of his lower-middle-class neighbors, is not confessing a snobbery but reflecting on his own moral decline when he recognizes a familiar name in a letter in The Times commenting on a great topic from a mean address. He responds "with enormous sympathy for the stirring of some chained and desperate spirit" (MM, p.11). Most telling is his relation to his fellow boarders who, presumably, shared his loneliness in a city so new and strange to them. Lacking names, they enter his recollections of his first days in London in "character" – a word that hardly ever appears in the novel without being set off in quotation marks, a stylistic tic that underscores how the word for him has been stripped of all but its social meaning: "the girl from Kenya; her man friend, a blond, vacant alcoholic incapable of extended speech and making up for this with a fixed smile and gestures of great civility; the smiling, mute Burmese student; the Jewish youth, tall and prophetic in black; the bespectacled young Cockney who had as much trouble with his two Italian mistresses … as with the police; the Frenchman from Morocco who spent all day in his room, kept to Moroccan temperature with a paraffin stove, translating full-length American thrillers at speed – he did one or two a month." Although he admits that it "was always good to see them familiar in all the unknown of the city," he nevertheless acknowledges that "this was how they always appeared: two-dimensional, offering simple versions of themselves" (MM, pp. 17–18). Naipaul is describing a uniquely cosmopolitan experience of anonymity and abjection in which familiarity, a precious psychological good in a city where so much remains unfamiliar, is purchased at the exorbitant price of self-simplification.

Between simple, one-dimensional versions of themselves and the unknown story they carry within them, these "familiar characters" live, narrowly.

As a genre, the novel has always reserved a special place, however narrow, and a special role for characters who either are or will become familiar to its readers primarily in two- rather than three-dimensional portraits. Indeed, flatness, the organization of character around a single trait or attribute, can be an extremely effective device for isolating peculiar adaptations that modernization has either created, encouraged, or made more visible. But Naipaul's two-dimensional mimic men and women occupy the narrow space between caricature and stereotype, both of which offer convenient, but misleading synonyms and analogies for flatness. Flat characters are energized by their (often comical) singularity, but neither caricatures and stereotypes, which trade in categories, nor idiosyncrasies can offer, much less advance any genuine understanding of what it means for the individual to be, and importantly, to *feel*, alive.

I am not quibbling here about the narcissism of small differences. The "flat" character retains the capacity, as Forster observed, to acquire rounder contours, a capacity routinely denied to the stereotype. The stereotype, as the literal origins of the word indicates, is typecast, pre-fabricated, and pre-assigned to solid and fixed forms. It thus expresses a more mechanical, standard, and less differentiated vision of human beings than the word character, which retains important associations with the art of engraving. This difference is dramatized in the way flat characters animate and enrich, while stereotypes can only dispirit, when they do not enrage, those branded and limited by them. Flat characters, as Forster remarked in calling attention to them, are not meant to compete with, much less replace resplendently round characters, about which they orbit like pale moons. Their primary function is to contribute to the novel's representation of multifarious life. Paradoxically, flat characters, with their heightened idiosyncrasies, insistent humors, and inflexible wills, are necessary to ensure that the world the novel creates is as fully "rounded" as possible; they bring not only variety, but comedy and sometimes pathos to the novel's carnivalesque display of human behaviors. Dickens's novelistic universe abounds in such characters, who in turn infuse even the most downcast, somber, and darkest of his fictions with the exhilarating impression of human life endlessly recreating and adapting itself, defying extinction, eluding capture and ingestion into the featureless, anonymous, indistinct, conforming multitudes.

But flatness may also serve more sinister designs when it ceases to be an expressive surface on which idiosyncrasy is etched in high relief and becomes primarily a defensive shield against scrutiny, including self-scrutiny. In such cases, a character flattened (by external force or internal pressures) can collapse into the stereotype, a state from which it is unlikely to recover. In the general leveling and bluntness of perception that ensues, everyone can begin to assume the look of a flat, stale, and unprofitable character. A kind of perceptual contagion may result, in which the character who either is or simply *feels* threatened by loss of distinction, begins "flattening" those beneath or beside him, becomes the agent as well as target of ridicule and prejudice.

In *The Inheritance of Loss*, Kiran Desai captures the circular and in this instance comically self-confirming logic of "flat" projection in a scene in which a group of Hindus amiably converse about the high birth rate of Muslims. Mrs Sen, a minor character briefly but pointedly described as not "among the class that reads Jane Austen," comments knowingly on this demographic fact:

> "With that Koran, who can be surprised? They have no option but to be two-faced."
>
> The reasoning, they all knew from having heard this before, formed a central pillar of Hindu belief and it went like this: so strict was the Koran that its teachings were beyond human capability. Therefore Muslims were forced to pretend one thing, do another; they drank, smoked, ate pork, visited prostitutes, and then denied it. Unlike Hindus, who needn't deny.[19]

Such reasoning at once unites and divides. Stereotyped thinking, of course, is notoriously good at doing both in the guise of making sense, however limited or distorted, of human beings who otherwise baffle and amaze, as well as frighten and repel us. Hence the exemplary figure of Mrs Sen, a one-woman chorus voicing the common feeling, sanctioned by tradition, that the very vices that Muslims and Hindus share are simultaneously enlisted to demonstrate the hypocrisy of the one and the candor of the other. Lola, the novel's young heroine who does belong to the class that reads Jane Austen, is made uneasy by this "vulgar and incorrect" reasoning, and Desai, a careful novelist steering clear of overt didacticism, leaves it to us to decide whether it is the vulgarity or the incorrectness of the opinion that offends Lola most.

The vulgar and incorrect stereotype is not a phenomenon confined to the hinterlands nestled just below the Himalayas on the Nepalese border, where half of Desai's novel is set. The other half takes place in Manhattan, a city where stereotypes proliferate and prove equally, if not more tenacious. They may even prove a greater "environmental factor" in determining how character is molded and perceived, for it is in the city novel that the casualties as well as seekers of modernity – with its riches and impoverishments, its promise of change, excitement, spectacle, pleasures, and cultural difference – converge and confront each other. We have become so accustomed, even addicted to the dynamism and spectacles of metropolitan life, that we are prone to forget, underestimate, or, more brutally, simply write off their human costs. We should feel a chill in that part of our spine that registers the approach of danger when we hear someone say or write with excitement rather than sadness that the city is the "real" or most lively character in a novel or a film. Such a remark disguises, and in worst cases, it exults in the diminishment or negligibility of human life. It endows the city with a reality that the city, as Naipaul insists, itself withholds from its more disadvantaged inhabitants. The immigrant experience of *Mimic Men* is repeated in novel after novel: how the great cosmopolitan cities of modernity threaten to monopolize reality, how human life correspondingly becomes less substantial, commanding less rather than more of our instinctive reverence. Cosmopolitanism, however spirit-expanding it promises to be, can also open up one more route to the nullity that Naipaul sees encroaching everywhere with the advance of a modernity that takes little notice and less care to preserve the traditions and sanctities of rooted, native life. As human characters struggle for a foothold, "the great city, so three-dimensional, so rooted in its soil, drawing colour from such depths" (MM, p.32) becomes the only enduring reality. In such grand and dazzling environments, new characteristics are acquired: the individual becomes more isolated, less morally robust, transparent to the point of invisibility (the peculiar form of non-existence Ellison chronicled with such lacerating, if baffled fury in *The Invisible Man*). No one *can* remain invisible in a village or small town – that is one of the things to be argued for as well as against knowable communities in which you are only too well known.

Naipaul describes and is clearly frightened by the way in which those who come to the city seeking self-enlargement and other forms of fulfillment find that they have instead

> lost some of our solidity; we were trapped into fixed, flat postures. And, in this growing dissociation between ourselves and the city in which we walked, scores of separate meetings, not linked even by ourselves, who became nothing more than perceivers: everyone reduced, reciprocally, to a succession of such meetings, so that first experience and then personality divided bewilderingly into compartments. Each person concealed his own darkness.... Little twinges of panic too, already. Not the panic of being lost or lonely; the panic of ceasing to feel myself as a whole person. The threat of other people's lives, the remembered private landscapes, the relationships, the order which was not mine. I had longed for largeness. How, in the city, could largeness come to me? How could I fashion order out of all these unrelated adventures and encounters, myself never the same, never even the thread on which these things were hung? They came endlessly out of the darkness, and they couldn't be placed or fixed. And always at the end of the evening the book-shaped room, the tall window, myself sitting toward the light or towards the mirror. (MM, pp. 32–33)

Novelistic character entails and requires ideas of largeness, magnanimity, expansiveness, generosity, all cognates for the increase of

Life. Naipaul's deracinated natives seek out cognates for the loss of largeness, the loss of the hope for largeness: titles like *The Mimic Men* and *Half a Life* report several unhappy outcomes of that quest. The feeling of halfness, which is quite a different sensation from feeling split in two, is a congenital condition for the Naipaulian character, a measure of its incompleteness. The Lawrentian injunction to become an "integral" being, what Naipaul, risking New Age cliché, calls a whole person, has been reduced to a panic reflex. Mimicry, as this passage implies, is the public manifestation of this panic reflex, a performance in which the mimic man tries to conceal, from himself as much as from others, that he exists between two darknesses, the darkness within and the darkness without. This is one terrible sense of what it means to live, narrowly.

The narrator's almost clinical detachment in reflecting on the remorseless process by which he is reduced to a fixed and flat personality may be read as a further sign of the dissociated existence the mimic man leads. But I think it is more likely that his flat affect is meant to suggest that the narrator, who writes retrospectively of the ordeals that formed his present reclusive character, has pierced the darkness and no longer rhetorically needs to mimic, in agitated pose or hysterical rhetoric, the panic he once felt. Two slight, but hopeful intimations gleaned at the end of this passage support this hope. One is the light, issuing from an unknown or undisclosed source, to which the narrator turns when he returns to his cell. By this light, he may find a way to push back the darkness, if not dispel it altogether (this is a fantasy that can irradiate the darkest time or place or culture; such fantasies fuel the prophetic imagination). The other is the mirror, emblem of his vocation as writer/metamir. The image he sees reflected there gives a human face to the disintegration and disorder of the postcolonial world in which few heroes or heroines can expect to become, in the sense George Eliot would have understood and championed, a complete person.

At first that face is a practiced one, fashioned to conform to preexisting notions of the colonial at ease with himself. Of course, it is the admission of the falsity and artificiality of that self-image that gives *The Mimic Men* its claim and authority as a "truthful" work of art. Let us linger over this paradox, which lies at the heart of Naipaul's and much other Native-Cosmopolitan fiction. In *The Mimic Men,* whose title announces the existential debacle its Third World natives strive to repair, the unnamed narrator devotes many pages to describing how he worked to create a "character": first "the dandy, the extravagant colonial, indifferent to scholarship" (MM, p.24), then the "politician and celebrant" of his native Trinidad. The novel is the long explanation of how he had tricked himself into mimicking a character and assuming a role for which he was temperamentally entirely unsuited. Self-deception is not, however, unique to mimic men, but in this unhappy breed self-deception and impersonation work so closely in the construction of character that it is difficult, as Naipaul's novel chronicles with great irony and patience, to discover what it would mean for such characters to become undeceived.

As writer/metamir the mimic man is even more deceptive, if also more entertaining, in passing off the imaginary experiences of other novels and films as genuine experiences of his own. Willie Chandron, the narrator of *Half a Life* is funny and touching in describing the ways in which as a young writer eager to create, but not yet knowing how newness comes into the world, he had put together stories from bits and pieces of books he had read or movies he had seen, borrowing, as it were, the Life he found outside his own experience as substitutes for the felt nullity of his own. Thus does the mimic man come to falsify his chosen subject – in this case, himself. The images he projects are nonetheless convincing enough to beguile readers, who in turn see themselves in them. One such reader, a young woman who writes him that "in your stories for the first time I find moments that are like moments in my own life, though the background and the material are so different," will become romantically involved with him, unaware that her secret sharer had borrowed and reworked such moments "from old Hollywood movies and the Maxim Gorky trilogy from Russia."[20]

As I noted in beginning this book, Eros always shadows the act of reading, prompting identifications and fantasies of spiritual connection where none do or can or arguably should exist. Such identifications, whether foolhardy, deluded, or, in certain sublime Quixotic instances, spiritually ennobling, suggest the power of those universal thought forms that, as Rushdie's Saleem reports, allow like to call out to like across the distances that separate them. But are backgrounds so disposable, a mere backdrop for the staging of universal moments? Are material differences in culture or experience so negligible? Psychologically perhaps, novelistically seldom to never. The novel is entrusted with describing and declaring the background against which character stands in varying degrees of high (or low) relief. What Naipaul's sardonic anecdote dramatizes is how the mimic man lacks a sufficient background from which he may emerge and acquire depth as a singular figure in his own right. His experience, the loss of a familiar world, is a common one in the postcolonial and millennial fiction of the past sixty years.

The title of Kiran Desai's novel of two families devastated by the dislocations that occur when traditional communities can neither absorb nor repel the influx of goods, ideas, and the manufactured longings disseminated through the global marketplace, recognizes this vanishing of the familiar world in the form of a paradox: *The Inheritance of Loss*. Desai is gesturing toward the experience of loss quite different from the emotional and moral devastation of *disinheritance*. Disinheritance, albeit a negative, often punitive or vengeful expression of the power – and responsibility – to bequeath goods and property to succeeding generations, has no quarrel with the concept and institutions, only with the recipients, of inheritance. The inheritance of loss, on the contrary, abandons the idea (and so the hope) of an inheritable material or cultural legacy, empties it of any meaningful human content. Desai's inheritors of loss – a young orphaned woman brought up in isolation by her disillusioned grandfather, a young man who emigrates to Manhattan to start a new life – are the desperate kin of the "bastard" child (Tom Jones) and orphans (Jane Eyre, Pip, Jude, Lolita!) of the classic novel. Like them, they have lost their place and indeed their claim to a materially and socially secure place in the sequence of generations. Unlike them, however, they begin the world with only one great and forlorn expectation: to witness, as powerless observers, the liquidation of their cultural heritage – its material goods and social traditions, its pieties, customs, ways of finding and assessing happiness. Without the power to reproduce and transmit its local traditions and indigenous values, cultures begin to deteriorate morally until they arrive, in Naipaul's bleak formulation, at "the final emptiness" (MM, 13). It was against this looming, all-extinguishing emptiness that Simone Weil pleaded when she warned that

> The future brings us nothing: it is we who in order to build it have to give it everything, our very life. But to be able to give one has to possess; and we possess no other life, no other living sap, than that treasure stored up from the past and digested, assimilated and created afresh in us. Of all the human soul's needs, none is more vital than this one of the past."[21]

The future may bring us nothing, as Weil insists, but we can bequeath it the sum of our own losses, a sum which is daily being tallied across the globe.

The New Man and the Native Cosmopolitan

The nullity of a future so drastically cut off from the past is made sensible in Naipaul's distressing account of "the special incompleteness of the Indian child, grandson of immigrants, whose past suddenly broke off, suddenly fell away into the chasm between the Antilles and India."[22] At first, Naipaul notes, "the child cannot grasp this loss as a catastrophe, since its dimensions are beyond his powers of comprehension." Once the child begins to accommodate the depth and finality of the catastrophe that has wiped out his cultural past (and all sense of how to recover it), grasping the dimensions of his loss becomes "difficult in another way":

> As soon as you tried to enter that idea it ramified. And it ramified more and more as our understanding grew; different people living for centuries where we now trod with our own overwhelming concerns; different people, with their own calendar and reverences and idea of human association, different houses or huts, different roads or paths, different crops and fields and vegetation (and seasons), different views, speeds, reasons for journeys, different ideas of the ages of man, different ideas of the enemy and fellowship and sanctity and what men owed themselves. (AWW, p.214)

Naipaul holds out no real hope that the chasm dividing the established traditions of the Past and the unsettled, often improvised ways of the Present can be bridged, even by the most determined and sympathetic act of historical imagination. If the Past survives, it can only be glimpsed through the general outlines of its evacuated forms – its human concerns, its reverences and sanctities, modes and rules for association, and ways of life of which we know nothing, except that they existed.

Naipaul is speaking for indigenous populations for whom history only seems to exist as a vast record of liquidations. Such people become aware that their own calendar, reverences, idea of human association, enmity, fellowship, and sanctity, in short their moral sense of what men – and women! – owe themselves, may in turn also vanish, leaving few, if any traces behind as the traditions which give continuity and substance to their everyday life are overlaid by the overwhelming concerns and different ideas, values, and aspirations of the next new man. "In this way," Naipaul concludes, "leaving aside the primary notion of cruelty, the idea of a wiped-out, complete past below one's feet quickly became almost metaphysical. The world appeared to lose some of its substance; reality became fluid. It was more natural to let go, to let the mind spring back to an everyday" (AWW, p.215). For those who inherit the emptiness rather than the fullness of the Past, the world "appeared to lose some of its substance." Naipaul is worried that the feeling for Reality itself is becoming atrophied as the world itself becomes more fluid, harder to grasp, more resistant to the creative and morally beneficent imposition of human meanings. This is one of the most important applications of "force" of character: to dominate one's environment, rendering it humanly and morally habitable.

Naipaul's solution for these metaphysical quandaries is novelistically worked out in the realm of daily life rather than in those upper regions of thought to which philosophers are better adapted. He finds his imaginative footing in the common, more solid ground of the everyday, in the local characters and places and customs of his homeland, to which he returns as a kind of prodigal as well as native son. There he begins to gather the substance, much of it perishable, that would restore solidity to his world.

Still, it is not easy to find what will satisfy him, even in the immediate data of everyday life. The aspiring writer of *A Way in the World* recounts how in his first "serious" fiction, he "didn't know what attitude to take to the character or setting," even though the character was imagined to be someone like himself. He almost reflexively tries "very hard in the colonial way to separate my character from his setting, to set him up a little higher," but can only accumulate pages documenting a day in the nonelevated, mundane life of his character, pages he refers to so self-dismissively that we know immediately that he had not managed to produce anything resembling a postcolonial *Ulysses* or *Mrs Dalloway* translated to the aboriginal/New World city of Port of Spain.

These pages are the seedpod, nonetheless, through which something new – in this case his own reclusive, ruminative, writerly character – comes into the world and having come, learns to survive there. Enigma, as one of Naipaul's more hypnotic titles informs us, accompanies this arrival of his newborn self. He writes of his self-emergence from the perspective of someone who has attained a new state of being that has not yet shed its mystery for him. "I had no idea what kind of person I was," the nameless narrator of *A Way in the World* confesses. "Writing should have helped me to see, to clarify myself" (AWW, p.86). However self-absorbed this may sound, Naipaul is writing in the culturally as well as psychologically generative tradition of modern self-portraiture. Moreover, as readers we would be much poorer without the discipline that attends such self-study, because his quest for self-clarity, like the adventures of Sir Walter Scott's heroic strivers with history, coincides with the great historical calamity that has overtaken him and because, as Lukács says of Scott's heroes, his attempt to clarify himself forces him to see, in concentrated form, both the positive and negative side of his Lamarckian metamorphosis into a new man, a "standard-bearer in good and in evil." Writing is a way to dispel confusion and to rectify the disorder that is his primary inheritance as a colonial. Indeed, Naipaul's fiction constitutes, in a quite peculiar and utterly original way, the memoirs of a survivor, a modern-day, cosmopolitan Crusoe who has survived the moral shipwreck of colonialism.

Shipwreck is a key word and image that recurs throughout *The Mimic Men*, the novel in which Naipaul chronicles the plight of "natives" left to drift in foreign cities or drown in the tumult of colonial misrule and revolutionary unrest. It is the verdict the narrator pronounces on his "own journey, scarcely begun, [which] had ended in the shipwreck which all my life I had sought to avoid" (MM, p.10). Later he isolates the word and endows it with a more specific existential content:

> Shipwreck: I have used this word before. With my island background, it was the word that always came to me. And this was what I felt I had encountered again in the great city: this feeling of being adrift, a cell of perception, little more, that might be altered, if only fleetingly, by any encounter. (MM, p.32)

The Mimic Men chronicles his own rescue from such a disastrous idea of a self that, as the name pitilessly exposes, has become purely imitative, a character from which we can apparently accept no original action or creative force. In retrospect he dismisses, with how deep an irony is open to question, the public, active phase in which he was "preparing" for life and by all accounts actually living it, to a parenthesis in some longer leisurely sentence written in the indefinite tense. Within this indefinite, convalescent time the spirit is germinating. Put another way, outside this parenthesis, Naipaul finds all the novelistic room he requires to assemble, greet, and create characters, including his own.

We can take the measure of this new man by comparing him to one of the many native characters whose existence Naipaul's cosmopolitan metamirs reflect with increasing and equal amounts of wonder and sadness. The one I personally remember most vividly is Leonard Side. He appears in the opening panel of *A Way in the World,* a section that telegraphs its concerns in its title, "Prelude: An Inheritance." Side, a "decorator of cakes and arranger of flowers" is in many ways the most disturbing figure for the educated, expatriate narrator, even as he is the least powerful, certainly the least important character in the novel, if importance is measured by social status, political power, or inner magnificence of character. He stands at the gateway of the novel, a monitory figure of the disinherited native, ignorant of his ancestry, the traditions that formed him, even the probable origins and history of his own name:

> He knew he was Mohammedan in spite of the picture of Christ in his bedroom. But he would have had almost no idea of where his ancestors had come from. He wouldn't have guessed that the name Side might have been a version of Sayed, and that his grandfather or great-grandfather might have come from a Shiva Muslim group in Indian. From Lucknow, perhaps; there was even a street in St James called Lucknow Street. All Leonard Side would have known of himself and his ancestors would have been what he had awakened to in his mother's house in St James. In that he was like the rest of us. (AWW, p.9)

Side's limited knowledge of himself and his ancestors makes him a particular kind of "representative" man. He is "like the rest of us" in inheriting a loss that is tribal and endemic and irreversible. Inheritance has become dematerialized; no longer an institution, nor a legal and moral concept, it has become the stuff of mystery:

> I can give you that historical bird's eye-view. But I cannot really explain the mystery of Leonard Side's inheritance. Most of us know

> where parents or grandparents come from. But we go back and back, forever; we go back all of us to the very beginning; in our blood and bone and brain we carry the memories of thousands of beings. I might say that an ancestor of Leonard Side's came from the dancing groups of Lucknow, the lewd men who painted their faces and tried to live like women. But that would only be a fragment of his inheritance, a fragment of the truth. We cannot understand all the traits we have inherited. Sometimes we can be strangers to ourselves. (AWW, p.11)

Strangers to ourselves. This prospect never occurred to Don Quixote, who declared even in defeat, I know who I am. And while we might protest that all of us are in some measure strangers to ourselves, the strangeness of which Naipaul speaks is more mysterious and intractable. It is a strangeness that can never be rectified by dogged research, including self-study, of the traits we have inherited since they are traits originating in traditions that have been lost to us, wiped out, in Naipaul's desolate colloquialism for the wholesale liquidations of our cultural inheritance.

This is the inheritance of loss that unites the disparate characters of the displaced person, the migrant, the voluntary expatriate, the Native Cosmopolitans of the present. And the future of character? Naipaul gives us a glimpse of a Lamarckian adaptation that is emerging as I write. It is a human possibility explored by the otherwise unprepossessing figure of De Groot, a university lecturer in African history whose father was a New Zealander and who "understood all attitudes in this part of Africa, and was detached from them all." We are told that De Groot himself divides the expatriate lovers of Africa into those who behave as if they are perpetual tourists and those who have "gone native": "the 'cob-cullers,' deer-hunters, people on an extended safari, and '*matoke*-eaters,' plantain-eaters, people who wanted to pretend for a while that they were Africans." The narrator remarks that De Groot

> saw himself as belonging to neither group (though he knew that to some people he looked like a *matoke*-eater). He never defined himself,

> but I think his attitude was that he was simply a man in his own setting, and fascinated by everything in that setting. In Africa, he had no special cause; people looking for man with a cause found him incomplete. (AWW, p.370)

We are, as George Eliot predicted, very far from the "complete man" fed by the rich blood of activity; yet in the character of De Groot we encounter someone who is perhaps equally remarkable, a man in his own setting fascinated by everything in that setting. In this simplification or silhouetting of character with in its setting we can discern the lineaments of the Native Cosmopolitan at home in his world, even as he is fascinated and estranged by it.

Earlier Naipaul had speculated, "Perhaps the philosophers were right. Perhaps below all the accidental things about people – birth, character, geography, history – there was something truer. That was what I had always felt about myself. Perhaps all men, if they were given a wise or rational liberty, became worthy of Plato's republic" (AWW, p.346). But we live in the world where birth, character, geography, history are more than the accidents that define human life; they are also fundamental, inescapable realities that possess a truth of their own. This book has examined one of those fundamental truths, foremost the truth of novelistic characters in all their indeterminacy and incompleteness and avidity for Life. If we look in and to them for a cause that answers or flatters our own, we will be disappointed. But if we look to them as examples of Nature striving to achieve its highest form, we will find not just the figures, but the promise of new Life.

Endnotes

1 Salman Rushdie, *Satanic Verses* (New York: Picador, 2000), p. 4. Hereafter S.
2 Richard Price, *Lush Life* (New York: Farrar, Strauss and Giroux, 2008), pp. 4–5.
3 Salman Rushdie, *The Wizard of Oz* (London: BFI, 1992), p. 14.

4 Nadine Gordimer, *Writing and Being* (Cambridge: Harvard University Press, 1995), p. 5.
5 Gordimer, 1995, p. 6.
6 Georg Lukács, *The Historical Novel* (London: Merilin, 1965), p. 38.
7 Thomas Pynchon, *The Crying of Lot 49* (New York: Harper and Row, 1990), p. 180.
8 Salman Rushdie, *Imaginary Homelands* (New York: Viking, 1991), p. 11.
9 Rushdie, 1991, p. 11.
10 Joseph Conrad, *Heart of Darkness* (New York: Penguin, 2007), p. 68.
11 D. H. Lawrence, "Study of Thomas Hardy," *Phoenix* (New York: Penguin, 1980), p. 414.
12 V. S. Naipaul, *A Way in the World* (New York: Vintage, 1995), p. 3. Henceforth AWW.
13 Anthony Appiah, *Cosmopolitanism: Ethics in a World of Strangers* (New York: W. W. Norton, 2007), p. xiv.
14 Martha Nussbaum, "Patriotism and Cosmopolitanism," *For Love of Country: Debating the Limits of Patriotism* (Boston: Beacon Press, 1996), p. 9.
15 Nussbaum, 1996, p. 9.
16 Appiah, 2007, p. vvii.
17 George Eliot, "The Modern Hep! Hep! Hep", *The Impressions of Theophrastus Such.* http://www.online-literature.com/george_eliot/theophrastus-such/18/
18 V. S. Naipaul, *Mimic Men* (New York: Vintage, 2001), p. 11. Hereafter MM.
19 Kiran Desai, *The Inheritance of Loss* (New York: Grove, 2006), p. 144.
20 V. S. Naipaul, *Half a Life* (New York: Vintage, 2002) pp. 116–17.
21 Simone Weil, *The Need for Roots* (New York: Routledge and Kegan, 1978), pp. 48–9.
22 V. S. Naipaul, *The Enigma of Arrival* (New York: Vintage, 1988), p. 157. Hereafter EA.

Index

Adam 8, 12, 48
Aeneas 31
Ahab, Captain 5, 26, 72
Albertine 7
Allen, Woody vii
Allworthy (*Tom Jones*) 57–9
Amadís of Gaul, 29, 31, 32, 45
Antigone 82, 90
Appiah, Anthony 164–6, 168
Archer, Isabel (*Portrait of a Lady*) 15, 16, 69, 74, 78–9, 83–6, 89, 115, 117–19
Aristotle 2, 4, 87
Aspects of the Novel vii, 10, 11, 72
Austen, Jane 18, 64, 67–8, 71, 76–7, 80, 172–3
Aziz (*A Passage to India*) 128, 131

Bakhtin, Mikhail 70–1
Balzac ix
Barnes, Jake (*The Sun Also Rises*) 152
Barthes, Roland 7, 86
Beckett, Samuel 7, 16, 86, 116, 123–4, 152
Bellow, Saul 108
Bergson, Henri 109
Bernard (*The Waves*) 108
Bernardo 13
Birkin, Rupert (*Women in Love*) 132
Bloom, Harold 38
Bloom, Leopold (*Ulysses*) 107, 126, 135, 137–8
Bloom, Molly (*Ulysses*) 137
Boethius 75
Borges, Jose Luis 101
Bovary, Madame vii, 26, 78, 88, 152
Bridehead, Sue (*Jude the Obscure*) 78

Briscoe, Lily 126
Brontë, Charlotte vii, 64, 79
Brontë, Emily vii, 64
Brooke, Celia (*Middlemarch*) 89
Brooke, Dorothea (*Middlemarch*) 74, 78, 89–93
Brothers Karamazov, The 5
Burke, Kenneth 126, 130
Burmese Days 152

Carey, Philip (*Of Human Bondage*) 151
Carlyle, Thomas 116, 118
Carmen 126
Casaubon (*Middlemarch*) 78
Celia (*Murphy*) 16, 17
Cervantes, Miguel ix, 35, 55, 60, 159
Chettam, Sir James (*Middlemarch*) 89
Christ, Jesus 41
Churchill, Frank (*Emma*) 68
Clare, Angel (*Tess of the d'Urbervilles*) 88
Clarissa 54, 78
Clèves, Princess of 61, 63
Clytemnestra 82
Coetzee, J. M. 54, 153
Confidence Man, The 25, 26
Conrad, Joseph 116, 153, 160
Copperfield, David 74, 78, 88
Crusoe, Robinson xii, 5, 17, 43, 44–54, 67, 77, 90, 102, 150, 164, 181
Crying of Lot 49, The 158
Cymbeline 125

Dalloway, Clarissa (*Mrs Dalloway*) 119–22
Danticat, Edwidge 153
Darcy, Fitzwilliam (*Pride and Prejudice*) vii
Darwin, Charles 99, 132, 151
De Groot (*A Way in the World*) 183–4
Dedalus, Stephen (*Ulysses*) 125–6, 135–7, 152, 155
Defoe, Daniel 44
Desai, Anita 153
Desai, Kiran 153, 172–3, 177
Dickens, Charles 3, 18, 71, 79, 88, 96–7, 128, 159, 172
Don Quixote x, 5, 30, 31–4, 36–43, 62, 82, 111–12
Dora (*David Copperfield*) 78
Dostoevsky, Fyodor 10, 18
Dubliners 137
Dulcinea (*Don Quixote*) 34, 41

Eliot, George 4, 64, 71–3, 78, 89–94, 108, 110–11, 167–8, 175, 184
Elliott, Anne (*Persuasion*) 76–7
Elliott, Rickie (*The Longest Journey*) 151
Ellison, Ralph 120, 140–1, 174
Emerson, Ralph Waldo 1, 5, 6, 17, 25, 27, 34, 46, 71, 83, 110–12, 150
Emile 45
Emma 67–73
Enigma of Arrival, The 178
Erikson, Eric 139
Estella (*Great Expectations*) 95
Ethical Characters 2
Eve 48
"Experience" 34
Eyre, Jane 74, 177

Fairfax, Jane (*Emma*) 68
Father Time (*Jude the Obscure*) 108

Female Quixote 54
Fielding (*A Passage to India*) 128, 131
Fielding, Henry 53–7, 59
Finn, Phineas (Palliser novels) 71
Flanders, Moll 47, 49, 61, 82–3
Flaubert x
Flaubert, Gustave 26, 99
Flory, James (*Burmese Days*) 151
Foe 54
For Love of Country: Debating the Limits of Patriotism 165
Forster, E. M. vii, viii, xii, 10, 11, 12, 72, 81, 128, 130, 134, 151, 171
Freud, Sigmund 8, 9, 95, 123
Friday (*Robinson Crusoe*) 52
Fuentes, Carlos 39

Gabler, Hedda 82
Gandhi, Mahatma 159
Garnett, David 132
Gaskell, Elizabeth 71
Genealogy of Morals 92
George, St 42
Gertrude 14, 15
Girard, René 30, 31
Godbole (*A Passage to India*) 128
Goodwood, Caspar (*The Portrait of a Lady*) 85
Gordimer, Nadine 6, 7, 8, 10, 12, 153, 155–6
Gorky, Maxim 176
Great Expectations 3, 94–8

Half a Life 175
Hamlet 13, 14
Hamlet 13, 14, 15, 26, 27, 38, 137
Hamlet, King 13
Hardy, Thomas 26, 71, 108, 152, 162–3
Harleth, Gwendolyn (*Daniel Deronda*) 78
Harlowe, Clarissa 54, 61, 64
Haven, C. Dexter 12
Havisham, Miss (*Great Expectations*) 96
Heart of Darkness, The 160
Heathcliff vii, 72–3
Helmer, Nora 82
Hemingway, Ernest 116, 152
Historical Novel, The 157
Humbert Humbert (Lolita) 7
Hyde, Mr 102, 108

Ibsen, Henrik 82
Icarus 136
Identity, Youth and Crisis 139
Imaginary Homelands 159
Impressions of Theophrastus Such, The 167–8
Inheritance of Loss, The 172, 177
Invisible Man 120, 140–1
Invisible Man 140–1, 174
Ishiguro, Kazuo 152

Jaggars (*Great Expectations*) 96
James the Moorkiller, St 42
James, Henry 15–16, 69–70, 85–7, 89, 101, 114–18
James, William 113–14, 122
Jane Eyre 83
Jekyll, Dr 100–2, 107–8
Jesus 99
Johnson, Samuel 19, 54, 55, 99
Jones, Tom 57–9, 152, 177
José (*Carmen*) 126
Joseph Conrad and the Fiction of Autobiography 7

Joyce, James 44, 46, 96, 125, 134–7, 152
Judas 52
Jude the Obscure 74, 152, 163, 177
Juliet 82

Kafka, Franz 18
Karenina, Anna 26
Keats, John 99
Kelly, Mr (*Murphy*) 16
Keywords 75
Kim 127, 130
Kim 127–8
Kingston, Maxine Hong 142
Kipling, Rudyard 127, 130
Kittredge, George 12
Knightley, Mr (*Emma*) 68, 70, 73
Kundera, Milan ix, x, 20
Kurtz (*Heart of Darkness*) 100, 160–1

Laertes (*Hamlet*) 13, 69
Lafayette, Madame de 61
Lahiri, Jhumpa 153
Lamarck, Jean-Baptiste 151, 157, 161, 164, 169, 181, 183
Lawrence, D. H. 7, 92, 131–5, 162–3, 175
Lennox, Charlotte 54
Levi, Primo 155–6
Literary Women 88
Locke, John 157
Lolita (*Lolita*) 177
Lord, Traci 12
Lukács, Georg 9, 157, 181
Lush Life 153–4
Lydgate, Tertius (*Middlemarch*) 74, 88, 90–4, 101, 108

Madariaga, Salvador de 33
Magwitch (*Great Expectations*) 95, 97
Malone 7, 152
Mann, Thomas x
Marcela 61–3, 82
Marlow (*Heart of Darkness*) 100, 160–1
Martin, St 42
Marx, Karl 45, 46, 91
Matthew, St 39
Maugham, Somerset 151
Mayor of Casterbridge, The 78, 80
McCarthy, Cormac 150
McDowell, Gerty (*Ulysses*) 152
Medea 82
Medusa and the Snail, The 110
Melville, Herman 25, 26, 27, 32, 38, 44, 61, 63, 100
Merle, Madame (*The Portrait of a Lady*) 83–5, 114–18, 120
Micawber, Mr (*David Copperfield*) 96
Micawber, Mrs (*David Copperfield*) 11
Middlemarch 71, 77–8, 89–94, 110
Midnight's Children 141, 155–62
Mill, John Stuart 4, 5, 74, 77, 80–1, 100
Millamant 82
Milton, John 26
Mimic Men, The 169–70, 173–6, 181
"Mirror Maker, The" 155
Moby Dick 72
Moers, Ellen 88
Molloy 152
Moor's Last Sigh, The 54, 159
Moore, Mrs (*A Passage to India*) 128–31

Moran 152
Morel, Mrs (*Sons and Lovers*) 131
Moretti, Franco 108
Morrell, Ottoline 7
Mrs Dalloway 118–23, 180
Mulligan, Buck (*Ulysses*) 135
Murdoch, Iris 73–4
Murphy 16, 123–4
Murphy 16, 17, 124

Nabokov, Vladimir 7, 35, 116
Naipaul, V. S. 54, 116, 152–3, 160, 163, 166–7, 169–70, 173–84
Napoleon 30
Native Son 163
Nausica 152
Need for Roots, The 178
Nietzsche, Friedrich 92–3, 98
Novalis, xi
Nussbaum, Martha 165

O'Hara, Scarlett 10
Odysseus 137
Oedipus 57, 162
Of Human Bondage 151
On Individuality and Social Forms 75–6
On Liberty and other Essays 4–5, 74, 80–1
Orlando 123
Orlando 34
Orlick (*Great Expectations*) 3
Orwell, George 80, 152
Osmond, Gilbert (*The Portrait of a Lady*) 16, 80, 115
Othello 125

Panza, Sancho 32–8, 40, 43
Passage to India, A 128–30
Paul, St 39, 42
Penelope 86, 137
Persuasion 76–7
Phaedra 82
Phillotson, Richard (*Jude the Obscure*) 78
Picture of Dorian Gray, The 100
Pip (*Great Expectations*) 3, 74, 88, 94–5, 97, 152, 177
Plato 61, 63, 99, 184
Plutarch 44
Poetics 3, 87
Polonius 69
Portrait of a Lady, The 15, 16, 79, 83–7, 114–15, 117
Portrait of the Artist as a Young Man 135
Price, Martin 59
Price, Richard 153
Principles of Psychology 113
Proust, Marcel x, 120
Pynchon, Thomas 158

Quested, Adela (*A Passage to India*) 128
Quijano, Don 28–9, 39, 51–2, 62, 151
Quixote, Don xii, 5, 10, 14–15, 26–43, 45, 52–3, 55, 61–3, 67, 73, 89–90, 99, 108, 111–12, 151, 153, 159, 177, 183

Ramsay, Mrs 126
Rawdon (*Vanity Fair*) 78
Remembrance of Things Past 120
Renan, M. 99
Return of the Native, The 71, 162
Richardson, Samuel ix, 54–5
Road, The 150

Robinson 54
Robinson Crusoe 45–54
Rochester 72
Roddice, Hermione 7
Rorty, Amelia 18
Rosalind 82
Roth, Philip 166
Rousseau, Jean-Jacques 44, 46
Roxana (*Roxana: The Fortunate Mistress*) 49, 61, 83
Rushdie, Salman 54, 141, 149–50, 153–9, 164–6, 177

S/Z 7
Said, Edward 7
Saleem, Sinai 141, 155–61, 177
Sallust 44
Sarn, Prudence (*Precious Bane*) 152
Sartor Resartus 116
Satan 26
Satanic Verses, The 149
Scott, Sir Walter 157, 181
Sebald, W. G. 116, 152
Seidel, Michael 50
Sen, Mrs (*The Inheritance of Loss*) 172–3
Sermon on the Mount, 39
Shakespeare, William 82, 125–6, 134, 137
Shandy, Tristram 52
Shandy, Walter 51
Sharp, Becky (*Vanity Fair*) 74, 83, 88
Side, Leonard (*A Way in the World*) 182–3
Simmel, Georg 75–6
Smith, Zadie 153
Sons and Lovers 131
Sorel, Julien (*The Red and the Black*) 29
Soul of Man Under Socialism, The 98–100
Spark, Muriel 54
Squire Western (*Tom Jones*) 57–8
Stackpole, Henrietta (*The Portrait of a Lady*) 85–6
Stendhal 29
Sterne, Laurence 54, 55, 60
Stevenson, Robert Louis 100–2, 108, 138
Strange Case of Dr Jekyll and Mr Hyde, The 100–2

Teresa, St 89–90
Tess of the *d'Urbervilles* 163
Thackeray, William 71, 88
Theophrastus 2, 9, 13
Thomas, Lewis 109, 123
To the Lighthouse 126
Toby, Uncle (*Tristram Shandy*) 60–1
Tolstoy x
Tolstoy, Leo 26
Tom Jones 54–9
Touchett, Ralph 15, 16
Tristram Shandy 55, 60–1
Trollope, Anthony 71

Ulysses 31
Ulysses 5, 125, 135–7, 152, 180
Unamuno, Miguel de 37, 43

Vincy, Rosamund (*Middlemarch*) 77
Vionnet, Madame 83
Vye, Eustacia (*The Return of the Native*) 26, 88, 162–3

Wakem, Philip (*The Mill on the Floss*) 151
Walsh, Peter (*Mrs Dalloway*) 122
Warburton, Lord (*Portrait of a Lady*) 79, 89
Waves, The 108
Way in the World, A 163–4, 167, 179–80, 182–4
Webb, Mary 152
Weil, Simone 178
Wentworth, Captain (*Persuasion*) 77, 79–80
Wilde, Oscar 73, 98–100
Wilkins, Mrs (*Tom Jones*) 55–6
Williams, Raymond x, 74–5
Woman Warrior, A 142
Women in Love 7, 132–4
Wood, James 17
Woodhouse, Emma (*Emma*) 64, 67–73, 76, 78, 89–90, 119, 152
Woolf, Virginia 20, 107, 118, 120–1, 123, 125, 127, 138
Wright, Richard 163
Writing and Being 6, 155

Yeobright, Clym (*The Return of the Native*) 162–3

Wiley The manufacturer's authorized representative according to the EU General Product Safety Regulation is Wiley-VCH GmbH, Boschstr. 12, 69469 Weinheim, Germany, e-mail: Product_Safety@wiley.com.

Printed and bound by CPI Group (UK) Ltd, Croydon, CR0 4YY

27/07/2026

02178777-0002